BLUEPRINTS
Primary English
The Writing Book

Pie Corbett

Stanley Thornes (Publishers) Ltd

Do you receive *BLUEPRINTS NEWS*?

Blueprints is an expanding series of practical teacher's ideas books and photocopiable resources for use in primary schools. Books are available for separate infant and junior age ranges for every core and foundation subject, as well as for an ever widening range of other primary teaching needs. These include **Blueprints Primary English** books and **Blueprints Resource Banks**. **Blueprints** are carefully structured around the demands of the National Curriculum in England and Wales, but are used successfully by schools and teachers in Scotland, Northern Ireland and elsewhere.

Blueprints provide:
- *Total curriculum coverage*
- *Hundreds of practical ideas*
- *Books specifically for the age range you teach*
- *Flexible resources for the whole school or for individual teachers*
- *Excellent photocopiable sheets – ideal for assessment and children's work profiles*
- *Supreme value.*

Books may be bought by credit card over the telephone and information obtained on **(01242) 577944**. Alternatively, photocopy and return this **FREEPOST** form to receive **Blueprints News**, our regular update on all new and existing titles. You may also like to add the name of a friend who would be interested in being on the mailing list.

Please add my name to the **BLUEPRINTS NEWS** mailing list.

Mr/Mrs/Miss/Ms _____

Home address _____

_____ Postcode _____

School address _____

_____ Postcode _____

Please also send **BLUEPRINTS NEWS** to:

Mr/Mrs/Miss/Ms _____

Address _____

_____ Postcode _____

To: Marketing Services Dept., Stanley Thornes Ltd, FREEPOST (GR 782), Cheltenham, GL50 1BR

First published in 1994 by:
Stanley Thornes (Publishers) Ltd
Ellenborough House
Wellington Street
CHELTENHAM GL50 1YW

Reprinted 1995 (twice)

A catalogue record for this book is available from the British Library.

ISBN 0–7487–1709–9

Typeset by Tech-Set, Gateshead, Tyne & Wear.
Printed and bound in Great Britain by Ashford Colour Press, Gosport.

CONTENTS

INTRODUCTION

The Writing Book is a structured and comprehensive bank of ideas, including 98 photocopiable copymasters designed to allow you to develop writing with primary-school children. It is concerned mainly with the compositional aspects of writing, rather than spelling, handwriting and punctuation. You will find a discussion of this approach at the start of the section on 'Teaching writing in the classroom' below.

This book covers all the types of writing that children need to undertake to meet the requirements of the National Curriculum in England, Wales and Northern Ireland, as well as the National Guidelines for English Language 5–14 for Scotland. You will find a detailed explanation of the coverage in 'National Curriculum links' on page xii.

The book has five main sections to provide complete coverage of all the key writing forms and skills. These are:

- 'Writing stories and poems' (imaginative writing in the Scottish curriculum)
- 'Writing for information' (functional writing in the Scottish curriculum)
- 'Writing from reading' (often called response writing)
- 'Writing from personal experience' (personal writing in the Scottish curriculum)
- 'Redrafting and proofreading'.

In addition you will find a clear discussion of strategies for teaching writing in the classroom, record keeping and assessment (the final redrafting section includes useful self-assessment sheets for use by the children, and a teacher's record-keeping sheet and accompanying prompt sheet to remind teachers of the key aspects of writing that need assessment), and a short bibliography of practical, straightforward books that will provide ideas for classroom activities. Since many teachers also like to link writing with topic work, a topic index has been provided.

Each of the five sections contains photocopiable copymasters, concise teacher's notes to accompany them and a bank of further ideas to get writing going. You will find that many real examples of children's writing have been included throughout. There are also occasional examples of the range and diversity of writing that can be generated with these classroom-tested ideas in the teacher's notes: these can be read to the class or used as further models or starting points to stimulate children's writing.

The copymasters are intended to be used across the whole primary age range and develop progressively within each section, beginning with ideas suitable for middle and top infants and becoming more and more difficult as the section goes on. Precise Key Stages have not been assigned to activities as their difficulty varies considerably from child to child and from class to class. Teachers will wish to use their own judgement as to what is appropriate for each child.

All the copymasters in this book are drawn from wide experience of successful classroom teaching, and the aim has been to provide a variety of approaches. You will find it useful to read the teacher's notes to get the most from each copymaster, but often you will have your own ideas about how to use the sheets. One of the advantages copymasters have over the traditional text book is that they can be written on: on many sheets pupils can underline, circle, edit, correct spellings and even cut up and reassemble. You will also find that many of the completed copymasters will make attractive classroom display material.

It is important to remember that developing writers should enjoy writing. The copymasters provide a set of activities that have already been proven in the classroom. Each copymaster will need to be introduced to the children with a clear explanation of the task required and the teacher will need to ensure that the work is carried out with care and commitment. Completed pieces of writing need to be shared and 'published' in displays or books. There is nothing like having a real audience to motivate writing!

TEACHING WRITING IN THE CLASSROOM ▶

Understanding the writing process

My brother is financial director of a large company which makes bricks and tiles. Quite often when we go to visit him at home I've seen him using his small hand-held tape-recorder to dictate a letter. No doubt, on his return to work, his secretary types up the letter for my brother to sign. Now, who wrote the letter? My brother *composed* the letter whilst his secretary *transcribed* it:

he made it up and his secretary wrote it down. Of course, handwriting and spelling (transcription) support the communication of meaning (composition) but these are two different skills and you could be good at one and not at the other.

There is no doubt that for many children the business of sitting down to write is a complex and difficult job. There is so much to attend to and get right:

Where does the date go? Can I get the letters on the line? How do you spell this word? What shall I say next? How big should the margin be? Should there be a full stop? Indeed, the complexity of the act of writing makes one wonder that children ever get going!

Part of the difficulty is that children believe that when we (as adults) sit down to write we manage to orchestrate all these problems perfectly, straight away, to produce beautifully written, perfectly spelt, well-composed writing that needs no attention or readjustment of any sort. In reality this is not so at all. An important feature of breaking down this myth involves teachers rediscovering the excitement they felt when they first became writers by writing again and sharing the struggles, the difficulties, the first drafts, the abandoned attempts and the successes of their own work with the children.

To make writing an easier task we can encourage children to focus first of all on the *composition* – on finding the right words and the right structure. They should not worry about the *transcriptional* issues until the written work is to be made public. Looking at writing in this way certainly eases the tension created by a child wanting to 'get it right' and avoids concentrating on the secretarial skills at the expense of making up anything worth saying. **This book concentrates on developing compositional aspects of writing.**

It is interesting how, when you ask children questions such as 'What is the most important thing to think about when you are writing?', many will say things like 'the spelling', 'getting the date in', 'the margin', 'writing on the line', 'the finger gaps', 'doing it neat' and so on. Ask your class this question and see where their focus lies. This sort of answer reflects the messages we have given children about what matters when we write and about what makes a successful piece of writing.

Another reason for considering the compositional and secretarial aspects as separate issues stems from a careful reflection on how adults write. From the 1970s onwards the growing trend of inviting writers and poets into schools began to move many teachers to consider whether there was anything to be gained from children not just learning to write, but actually becoming writers. These teachers learned from working with writers various approaches to writing that might be adapted usefully to the classroom – brainstorming, revising, proofreading, publishing and ensuring an audience for writing were all ideas that reflect the ways in which adult writers work.

A consideration of how we write as adults underpins much of our present thinking about the possible ways children might develop as writers – this laced with careful note of what works for children and what does not. 'Good Primary Teachers pay attention to the process of writing, developed from a knowledge and understanding of the practice of experienced writers (including themselves); they are then able to provide classroom practices which allow children to behave like real writers' (*English for Ages 5 to 16* June 1989, para. 3.13). This belief was clearly a cornerstone of the original Programme of Study.

In both the Northern Ireland and Scottish documents a similar approach is required – emphasis is placed on the process of writing, the compositional and secretarial aspects and the importance of children writing for genuine audiences. The 'consultation report' that came from the NCC in September 1993 still hinges the approach to writing around the same notion. The strands in this document clearly identify the same concerns and beliefs.

This approach has lead to a view of the writing process that may be illustrated by the following diagram:

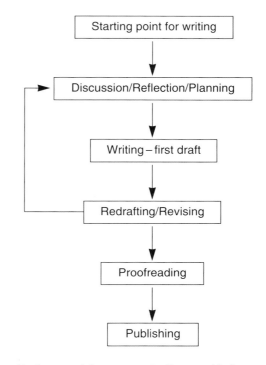

Each part of the process is discussed below.

Providing starting points

Children need to write for a variety of purposes and audiences, in a variety of different situations, so that they can have experience of matching style and content to audience and purpose. Some of these starting points will be determined by the teacher but there will also be opportunities for some to be determined by the children themselves. They will write letters, notes, diaries, newspapers, poems, stories and so on to friends and other children, for parents, the teacher, granny, even the school cook!

The copymasters provide a wide range of starting points and cover all kinds of writing. The first section looks at literary writing – stories and poems. The next section deals with the many forms of information writing. It touches upon diaries, letters, captions, labels, instructions, rules, recipes, opinions, adverts, greetings, lists, news, signs and reviews. The third section looks at writing in response to reading stories, poems and information, which is commonly referred to as response writing. Finally there is a section of ideas concerning personal writing based on children's own experiences.

Younger children will need to have the opportunity to play at writing and to imitate. They will need to see the teacher write in front of them on a regular basis. They will be motivated to write by the provision of writing opportunities in the home corner and writing area. Often just providing a postbox or some home-made booklets is sufficient stimulus.

The home corner

Older children need starting points that arise from their own reading and their own lives. The subjects chosen need to be manageable, interesting and challenging. They need to be rooted in something that the child knows and has something to say about. The subjects should also invite children to play with language and ideas.

Discussion, reflection and planning
Once a starting point has been thought of its function and form need to be considered and finalised: what is its purpose, who is it for, what needs to be said, what is the best format? Some initial planning and discussion of ideas and approaches may be useful. This could include considering how much time is needed and who will carry out which task. These early discussions may need to be recorded and noted.

As with any form of worksheet a copymaster will be unlikely to succeed on its own. It will need introducing and the children will need to use it within the framework of the writing process. Careful reading of the teacher's notes will assist you in this.

Moving straight into writing about an experience may prove to be difficult for many children (and adults). There is something to be said for leaving time for reflection and discussion before writing. This may provide an opportunity for writers to think around the subject, mull it over, sift ideas, discover their own viewpoint, see a way into the writing, listen to and use vocabulary, and discover what the experience meant for them. This early stage may act as a sort of linguistic bridge between the abstract experience and the concrete act of tussling with words on the page. To assist in this stage various tactics may help:

Discussion The traditional discussion about the subject lead by the teacher. In this the teacher often asks questions to get the children to 'rehearse' the sorts of things they might 'say' in their writing. This can also be done by putting the children into pairs or small groups to talk through or explain what they are thinking about saying and what they know about the subject, or to try out their story.

Image making Activities such as drawing, model making, painting, printing and so on can help children to focus upon a given starting point, internalise much of the detail, use appropriate language in passing talk and begin to discover what the image means to them. This might also apply to making music, dramatic activity, dance, mime and so on.

Brainstorming This can be carried out as a class, group, paired or individual activity. The aim is that those involved contribute as many ideas as possible over a short period of time. Anything is accepted. After seven or eight minutes the group then reflect on the various ideas, and begin to sift and organise them. This is a useful technique for quickly sharing thoughts and can unlock new ideas and stimulate creative thinking.

Brainstorming

Writing the first draft
Once there has been some consideration of the subject matter and appropriate planning then the initial composition begins. At this stage the child has to start to grapple with making up what to say as well as the problems of getting the words down on the page. A number of strategies can be used to help writers focus upon the composition and to make the transcription easier such as:

Scribing The teacher, another adult, a mature writer or another group member jots down what is being said.

Wordprocessor Pupils write directly on to the wordprocessor or an adult types for them. This is very useful for children who have difficulties in achieving a flowing handwriting style, because it enables them to produce a neat and legible copy. Research has shown that this has improved such children's self-confidence as writers and increased the amount they write.

Taping A small tape-recorder can provide the opportunity to come up with ideas and record them spontaneously, before any transcription is necessary.

Inventing spelling   Encouraging children to invent their own spellings or to use a spelling line means that the compositional flow can be maintained. (A spelling or magic line is where a child may only be sure of how to spell the beginning of a word and uses a line to represent the letters they are unsure of. In this way a word like 'dog' might be written as 'd – –'. The correct spelling can be inserted later on.) The original National Curriculum documentation highlighted the importance of children being 'helped to be confident in attempting to spell words for themselves without undue dependence on the teacher.'

(I bought a new truck. It is [my] best one. It can drive over my hand.)

Invented spelling

Burst writing   This technique involves putting pressure on the writer to write as much as possible in a very short period of time without paying attention to the conventions of spelling, punctuation and so on. This can release a sudden and surprising flow of ideas and is a useful way of overcoming writer's block.

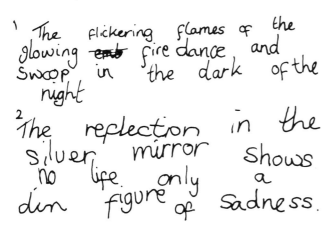

Burst writing

Redrafting and revising

If it is appropriate, the writing can be redrafted with a view to developing and reshaping the initial draft to make the communication more effective. Of course, you do not need to redraft a shopping list or notes, but a story or important letter may need such treatment. When redrafting the focus is still upon the compositional aspects, making sure that the piece of writing states what was intended in the best possible way. In order to redraft effectively it helps if the writer can see the piece of writing from a reader's viewpoint. Redrafting can be carried out:

With the teacher   The teacher needs to sit alongside the pupils – individually, in groups or with the whole class – and talk through ideas for redrafting and reshaping writing, and changing, deleting and adding words, giving reasons for why certain changes make the piece of writing more effective.

In pairs   Pupils can be paired together to redraft work, taking it in turns to act as editors for each other. **Copymaster 83** (Response partner) provides useful guidelines for this approach.

In groups   When redrafting it is useful to get a reader's response. Story circles or topic groups can listen to each other's work in progress and offer advice on what seems to work well and what does not.

With teacher demonstration   Writing in front of the class using a flip chart, OHP or blackboard provides a chance to discuss revisions to work.

With the whole class   When reading children's work aloud the teacher can ask the children to identify the areas in the writing that are effective and that they enjoy, as well as the areas they think need development.

In the 'Redrafting and proofreading' section there are copymasters that give practice in revising stories and poems. When using these note that the writing and redrafting process can lead to various problems if not handled sensitively:

* There is the danger that children will change a few spellings and then write up their work neatly believing this to have been 'redrafting'
* There is no fixed number of drafts
* Not every piece needs to be redrafted
* Not all children redraft in the same way – the process has to be viewed flexibly.

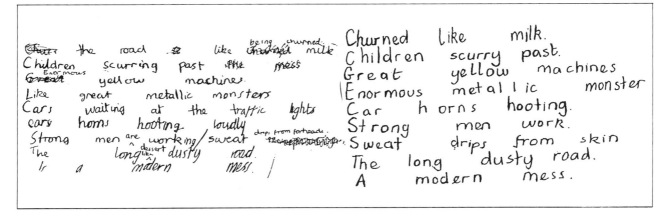

First draft   *Final copy*

Proofreading

Once the work has been redrafted and the writer has decided that it is going to be 'published' – as part of a display, in a scrapbook, as a book in its own right or in a class anthology – then the proofreading process needs to begin. It is at this stage that pupils check for incorrect spellings and punctuation, and decide upon layout and presentation. It should be made clear that all these considerations are important because they help to communicate swiftly and clearly. The final product should be written in 'best' handwriting or typed, out of respect for the reader. There are copymasters in the final section 'Redrafting and proofreading' that concentrate on proofreading for spelling and punctuation, and consider the layout and organisation of writing.

Publishing

The final product should be shared with appropriate audiences that may well include friends and family. It should also be assured a place in the class library. At this point the purpose of writing should now become clear – to entertain, inform, persuade, and share thoughts and feelings.

Published books

Keeping the writing process flexible

Not every piece of writing needs to follow this pattern. Diary entries, personal reflections, notes, reminders, impressions, logs, writing used as a way of learning or thinking aloud and exploratory writing may not need to move through these stages. Some pieces of writing that we thought would lead to publication have to be discontinued – learning about writing also involves learning when to decide to abandon pieces that never get off the ground. It is also important to be quite clear that although I have outlined a writing process above, no two writers are comfortable using exactly the same strategies. Children need access to a variety of strategies and approaches, and they need to explore their own ways of becoming effective as writers.

If you watch children closely as they write and ask them what they are doing, you discover, for instance, that they all redraft in slightly different ways. Some children redraft in their minds *before* they put a word down, some redraft *as* they write. Some write a few words and

```
                    The Burning Bush.

The bush blazed, brightly before Moses.
A voice came to him.
Take off your shoes said he.
Who are you? Said Moses.
I am the God of this mountain said he.
Take off your shoes for this is Holy ground.
Moses came nearer no more.
He took off his shoes and knelt down before the bush.
The bush blazed like the white inside of the sun.
And yet Moses could see that the bush was unchanged.
Then God spoke one single word!
His name.
And power from God poured into Moses
As wine filling a cup.
*****
*****
```

'Best' work

then make changes, some write whole sections and then go back over them, and others write the whole passage before they go back to redraft. Personally, I like to use a variety of the above strategies at different times! Having fixed expectations would be akin to expecting every child to learn to talk or read in exactly the same way. This means that we need to introduce and demonstrate various ways of working, using the process described above as a guiding framework within which children can write.

As you can see this process will take time. What is envisaged by the National Curriculum is a situation where we ask our pupils to do less writing, but ensure that what we do is more meaningful, more purposeful and is brought to a conclusion that allows every child a full opportunity to say what they want to say and to capture their thinking on the page. At the heart of this approach is the recognition that much of the thinking and work can be done by the children, that many of the decisions can be made by the children, that often the children should decide what they will write about and how, and that children should be taught to reflect critically upon their writing, using appropriate vocabulary in order to improve its effectiveness.

The teacher will have to consider carefully a number of key decisions:

- How to find reasons for writing which are purposeful, meaningful and act as an invitation to engage with a written task. This may mean establishing a task that the teacher suggests or providing opportunities for the children to negotiate their own writing tasks
- What sorts of support and advice the variety of children will need in class
- How the writing will be published and who the audience will be
- What sort of process will be used and what needs to be organised to carry out the writing task successfully.

The copymasters will provide a backbone for developing writing ideas and redrafting and proofreading skills. Many of these ideas will need to be reinforced and built upon in the classroom using principles similar to the ones outlined above.

RECORD KEEPING AND ASSESSMENT

Each child will need some form of on-going profile to act as a record of achievement, showing the child's development across the primary years. The profile will be contributed to by the child, the parents and the different teachers. A complete profile should include:

- Factual details – such as medical records
- Teachers' observations – notes made in different situations
- Samples – a collection of examples that act as tangible evidence of development with teacher's notes attached
- Reflections – the child's own comments on progress made and future targets, as well as comments by parents.

The on-going use of the profile should enable the children to have an idea of their own development, ensure that parents are kept informed and can contribute to children's progress. It should also assist the teacher in planning appropriate teaching.

Such on-going records can become too bulky and time consuming to be of any use. Some schools have become bogged down with vast sheets covered in ticks that, at the end of the day, seem to tell us little about the child. It has to be remembered that the Level Descriptions/Statements of Attainment are only a very limited view of what we are hoping to develop in children. They are the more objective indicators, but development in writing has many other signposts en route which teachers will look for. In the Cox Report it was stated that 'the best writing is vigorous, committed, honest and interesting. We have not included these qualities in our statements of attainment because they cannot be mapped on to levels. Even so, all good classroom practice will be geared to encouraging and fostering these vital qualities' (June 1989). Considering the new Level Descriptions/Statements of Attainment, this comment becomes even more important to bear in mind.

Schools need to develop an approach that is useful, practical and informative. If evidence is gathered over a period of time this will provide a picture of what the child can do in a range of situations, and so enable teachers to confidently state at what level the child is working. It is important to remember that it is a child's *general* performance over a period of time that suggests a level of attainment, not one individual piece of work. A useful summary is contained in the Non Statutory Guidelines published in June 1990 in the chapter on 'Gathering evidence of achievement'. The annual guidelines for assessing writing at the different Key Stages give important guidance on the criteria to be used for deciding when a child has reached a level of attainment.

The writing conference
In order to build an on-going picture of the child's development and to use this information directly to move the child forward, teachers will need to hold regular writing conferences with children.

The writing conference is an opportunity to focus upon a child's writing development. The teacher may want to focus upon one particular piece of writing or perhaps discuss a folder of writing. Some possible approaches include the following:

- Let the child talk about their favourite piece
- Ask about the child's approach to writing i.e. how they set about the task
- Ask about the intended audience, purpose and form
- Get the child to take you through the various drafts telling you why changes were made. Try to get a window on to the child as a writer
- Find out if there is a point of growth you can identify together, a next development to work towards.

Comments and notes could focus upon the following:

1 Child's response
2 Content
3 Conventions – spelling/punctuation/handwriting
4 Process – planning, redrafting, proofreading and publishing
5 The next development.

Discuss any agreed point(s) and make this a focus for the child. Be careful about offering rules and definitions as a way of helping. Rules are abstract in nature and can only be understood in relation to a developing competence. *Show* the child how something is done – teach by illustration not definition. Look for patterns in errors and pinpoint any common, gross errors to work upon. Alternatively, ask the child what they would like to concentrate upon. Where useful, relate the child's writing to aspects of the reading the class has been doing.

Note down children's own responses to the selected piece or let them write a short note to go with it. Record the context – how the writing came about, who helped – and what this demonstrates about the child's growth as a writer.

Chosen pieces might be placed in the child's folder as being representative or interesting. They will need to have the note attached giving the context, teacher's and child's comments. The teacher's notes might indicate why the writing has been chosen and any aspects of the Statements of Attainment that this demonstrates.

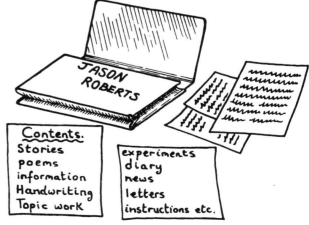

A child's folder

ix

Date	Comments	Recommendations
21/1/94	J. read his story to me - fluently. Well structured - interesting ending. Re-drafted together.	J. to focus on finding engaging beginnings plus checking for full stops.
19/2/94	Looked at J's diary. Uses wide vocabulary. Full stops becoming a habit!	Proofread for spellings.

Teacher's notebook

A record of the discussion should be kept in order to build up a supportive picture of the child's development as a writer and any agreed recommendations. A checklist in a teacher's notebook might look like the example above.

Copymaster 86 (My writing) or **Copymaster 96** (Self-assessment) can be used by the children to assess their

development over the course of a term or year. **Copymaster 97** (Writing record) can be used as a record sheet for writing conferences. **Copymaster 98** (Writing record prompt sheet) is designed to act as an aide memoire to teachers, highlighting key aspects of writing that should be noted.

Writing.

When I start to write a piece of writing I always build on a central idea, I prefer to work in quietness. If the piece of writing has to be good then I'm always concentrating. First of all I jot down ideas then I arrange them into the piece of writing. I then start to change words, I change non-interesting words for interesting ones. Make your work eye-catching and set it out so it looks good. Check for spelling mistakes. Never waste a good word, always try and fit it in. I like to read others work and grasp ideas from it. Look at ideas from all sides and find their best meaning and use. Use words that fit well in the piece of writing. Never stop concentrating, sometimes it helps to discuss your ideas with a friend.

Childs' comment on writing

x

NATIONAL CURRICULUM LINKS

Types of writing	Copymasters
Acrostic:	38
Adverts:	55
Aliteration:	22
Assessment:	97, 98
Audience:	56, 5
Bookmaking:	84
Book reviews:	54
Calligrams:	27, 28, 36
Captions:	44
Choosing words:	79
Contents:	62
Descriptions:	21, 23, 24, 30, 66
Diary:	13, 73, 76
Glossary:	62
Instructions:	52
Invitations:	45, 85
Labels:	16, 34, 72
Layout:	56–8
Letters:	46, 47, 59, 85
Lists:	41, 58, 65
Menus:	32
Messages:	14
Newspapers:	50, 51, 53, 61
Paragraphs:	56, 90, 95
Personal experience:	24, 68, 71–5
Planning:	3, 11, 19, 60
Proofreading:	83, 90, 95
Punctuation:	78, 83, 90, 95
Rapping:	40
Recipes:	42, 43
Redrafting:	77, 80, 81, 83, 88, 89, 92–4
Self-assessment:	86, 96
Sequencing:	1, 8, 10, 18, 35, 58, 59, 64
Signs:	48
Story endings:	7
Story grammar:	5, 20
Story openings:	2, 85
Story telling:	15, 63, 67
Traditional tales:	6, 9, 18, 81, 90
Word play:	25–8, 31, 33, 36, 37, 39, 69, 70

BOOKLIST

Catapults and Kingfishers, Pie Corbett and Brian Moses, Oxford University Press (1986).
A teaching handbook of ideas for poetry writing. Also a description of running a poetry writing session.

My Grandmother's Motorbike, Pie Corbett and Brian Moses, Oxford University Press (1990).
A teaching 'storehouse' of ideas for story writing covering the whole primary range plus a description of how to organise and run story writing sessions.

Does It Have to Rhyme?, Sandy Brownjohn, Hodder & Stoughton (1980).
Poetry writing ideas.

In Tune with Yourself, Jennifer Dunn, Morag Styles and Nick Warburton, Cambridge University Press (1987).
Poetry writing ideas and discussion of the teaching approach. Practical advice.

BP Teachers' Poetry Resources File for Primary Schools, The Poetry Society, 22 Betterton Street, London WC2H 9BU (1992).
Practical ideas in a loose-leaf file written by poets that visit schools. Updated with new articles each year.

Word Games and *More Word Games*, Sandy Brownjohn, Hodder & Stoughton (1985).
Lively approaches to developing word interest through writing and reading activities.

The Essential Guide to Poetry, David Orme, Folens (1992).
A lively collection of well-tested poetry ideas.

Did I Hear You Write?, Michael Rosen, André Deutsch (1989).
An interesting account of this popular poet's work in schools with plenty of ideas for poetry and personal writing.

TOPIC INDEX

WRITING STORIES AND POEMS

This section is designed to help children develop their ability to write stories and poetry. Children are invited to write individually, in pairs or in small groups, and in this way be influenced by each other as writers. There are activities to assist children in considering the sequence of a plot; that highlight story beginnings and endings; that emphasise planning and the consideration of setting, characters and situation before beginning to write; and that explore the importance of developing character, adding detail and using the solution of a dilemma as a storyline. Many of the copymasters act as imaginative writing stimuli.

The poetry activities highlight the importance of carefully selecting ideas and words. There are copymasters that encourage close attention to using the five senses, and to balance this there are activities that rely upon playing with words and ideas in a fun way. Writing poems as shapes is introduced as well as using rhyme.

STORIES

Copymaster 1 (Shopping tale)
Working in pairs, the children should look carefully at the sequence of pictures on **Copymaster 1**. They should then decide which order the pictures should go in. They could cut them out and re-order them, or number them on the page. The pictures could be stapled together and made into a small booklet.

Copymaster 2 (Starters)
The children read and choose which 'starter' they would like to use. Before they begin writing encourage the children to work in pairs. They should tell their partner what the story will be about, who is in it, where it is taking place and what will happen. Alternatively, they could draw their story as a sequence of pictures.

Copymaster 3 (Story questions)
The children should discuss with a partner and then fill in their answers to the questions. In this way it is expected that some planning will have occurred before children write their story.

Copymaster 4 (Supposing stories)
Many stories are based around the notion of 'What would happen if …' or 'Supposing …'. Use the opening lines on the copymaster to generate writing or to create more funny situations around which the children might write stories.

Copymaster 5 (Story builders)
Get the children to choose a main character, a place and an event to start their story going. They could cut out their choice and stick them into their story as illustrations.

Copymaster 6 (Fairy tale headlines)
The children have to complete the stories in the newspaper by cutting out the headlines and illustrations, sticking them on to a separate piece of paper and writing their accounts underneath.

Copymaster 7 (Endings)
The children could write the story that goes with the ending of their choice, working individually to begin with and then sharing their stories in pairs or small groups once written. They might then make up endings of their own and swop them. The children will probably need to have some time to talk about their story first, with the teacher or a partner, or to draw the action in cartoon form before writing as an aid to composition. Very small children could draw the sequence of the story and the teacher could then write it down.

Copymaster 8 (The magic box)
The story on this copymaster is being told through drawings. The children can tell each other how they would finish the story and fill in the empty boxes with their own pictures to show the end of the tale.

Copymaster 9 (Trolls)
This copymaster leaves space for the story shown to be added to and also leaves space for pictures. The story could be continued on further sheets, with the children weaving their writing and illustration together.

Copymaster 10 (Octopus story)
On each tentacle of the octopus there is a sentence from the start of a story. The children cut out the tentacles and put the sentences into the right order. This story may then be continued on further sheets.

Copymaster 11 (Story flow chart)
This copymaster is just a series of blank boxes linked together as for a flow chart. The flow chart can be used as an aid to planning. The children can either draw in the boxes or write briefly what happens next. Such a planner is also useful to ensure that key facts are not forgotten or that a sequence or process is in the right order.

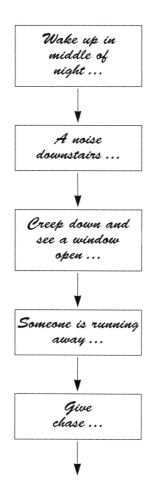

Wake up in middle of night ...

↓

A noise downstairs ...

↓

Creep down and see a window open ...

↓

Someone is running away ...

↓

Give chase ...

↓

Copymaster 12 (Expedition 1)
Put the children into pairs or small groups. They are going on a treasure-hunting expedition but can only carry 10 kilograms between them. They should decide which ten items they will take.

Copymaster 13 (Expedition 2)
The map on the copymaster was found in the attic by one of a group of explorers and is very old. It shows an island where hidden treasure is buried. The story of the explorers' adventure is written as a diary, the first page of which is on the copymaster. Get the children to read the map and diary entry carefully and then continue the story in the same style.

Copymaster 14 (Messages)
The children should complete the empty and half-torn messages. Working in pairs or groups, they could share each other's ideas, pretending that they have found one of these messages. They could then write a story that includes this message.

Copymaster 15 (Bare bones)
This copymaster contains the bare bones of the beginnings of three stories. Put the children into pairs. First they have to help each other tell the stories, adding in detail and fleshing out the bare bones so that the brief reports of what happens become stories. The children could then move on to writing down the versions they have practised.

Copymaster 16 (Potion stories)
Get the children to complete the rest of the bottles' labels with magic potions. They should then write a story of what happens when they – or their friends – accidently swallow one of the potions. (Please give the usual warning and reminder to children not to drink from odd bottles, etc.)

Copymaster 17 (Magic wishes)
This copymaster can be used by children working individually or in pairs to record a secret wish – to change something, become something, acquire a super power and so on. All the wish boxes on the copymaster are filled in by each child/pair. Each wish is cut out and placed in a hat, out of which every child chooses one. The children write the story of what happens when they rub a magic cola can and a genie pops out to grant the wish they have chosen.

Copymaster 18 (Dustbin story)
A writer has accidently torn up and thrown into a dustbin the first part of a story. Working individually the children should cut out the different fragments and piece together the story. Then, in pairs, versions should be compared. Working on their own children should then continue the story. They should write into the rest of the story a pig that sings, a bad fright and three bags of gold.

Copymaster 19 (Story skeleton)
Written on to the skeleton are a number of key words from a story and there are spaces where extra words can be added in. The children complete the skeleton with special words that they would like to use and then have to write down their story. Stories should be read aloud to consider the differences.

Copymaster 20 (Story stealer)
Tell the children that the story stealer has a huge trunk into which all the stories that you know have been placed. The stories have become completely muddled up. The children should use the chart to jot down titles of stories they know, settings, main characters, events and endings. Remind the children in discussion of traditional tales as well as stories shared in school. They should then circle one part of each column to make up a mixed bag of ingredients which should be used to write a new story.

POEMS

Copymaster 21 (Rainbow poem)
The children should use the rainbow shape to write a sentence for each colour. They should begin by colouring in the key that shows the order of the colours. They then have to think of one thing to describe for each colour and write the sentence or phrase into the rainbow space. For instance:

'Chunks of butter on my bread' (yellow)
'Oranges are rough to feel' (orange)
'A cut finger' (red).

Copymaster 22 (Counting poem)
The children should read the poem carefully. What do they notice about the sounds? They should now use the opposite half of the page to try writing their own counting poem, making the words sound the same if they can. This is an early introduction to alliteration.

Copymaster 23 (Listen)
This copymaster could be used on a school outing or for writing outside the classroom – in the playground, on the street and so on. The children use the sheet to jot down the different sounds they can hear. Back in the classroom this sheet is then used as the basis for a 'Listen' poem. You may wish to begin the writing session by reading the children this example, written after a visit to a busy street:

Listen,
can you here the bus grumbling by?
Listen,
can you hear the milk float rattle?
Listen,
can you hear the jet roar overhead?
Listen,
can you hear the police car's siren wailing?
Listen,
can you hear the shoppers' feet clacking?
Listen,
can you hear the cars' engines grinding?
Listen,
can you hear the distant train toot?
Listen,
can you hear yourself think?

Copymaster 24 (I am afraid)
The first few boxes on the copymaster have drawings of frightening things happening. The children fill in the empty boxes with their own pictures of frightening things, adding labels if they can write. Working from these drawings, the children could write a list poem as in the following example:

I am afraid of scary spiders.
I am afraid of people who shout at me.
I am afraid of lions that could eat you.
I am afraid of when it is dark.

Copymaster 25 (Magic stocking)
The idea of the magic stocking is that you could have any present you would like in it and whatever it is can be made out of anything! Use the lists on the copymaster to begin getting ideas for a 'Magic' poem. Children should circle an item from the present list then draw a line to what it could be made of. Try to encourage the children to remember that it is a 'Magic' poem and that the more unusual the combination the better. For instance a doll made of plastic is boring but a doll made of sunbeams may be rather special! Once the children have chosen they can then write up their poem, borrowing the same format as this example and adding their own ideas.

In my magic stocking
I would like –
a doll made of white clouds,
a book made of flames,
a shell-suit made of banana skins,
a troll made of roof tiles,
a pair of ballet shoes made of butterfly wings,
a chocolate bar made of sausages,
a secret made of washing-up water,
a playground game made of liver,
a tie made of electricity…

Copymaster 26 (Crazy wishes)
This poem is similar to the 'Magic' poem above in that the idea is to dream up the most ridiculous and impossible wishes. I have begun by listing a few such wishes on the copymaster and the children should read mine and then continue the list.

Copymaster 27 (Sea word-picture)
This copymaster shows a seaside picture. The children have to write carefully on to spaces on the copymaster words that describe the different things shown. So, they may write 'jagged' in the space on the rocks or 'soft' in the space on the sand.

Copymaster 28 (Bonfire calligram)
A calligram is a picture that is made up of words. In this calligram the children are given the faint outline of a bonfire and some fireworks. The children should write appropriate words or sentences over the outline to actually create the picture, so that they are 'drawing' with the words.

Copymaster 29 (Animal poem)
I have written out half of this poem about animals but have left the children to try to find rhyming words to complete each verse. Children could then go on to think of their own animals and rhymes to accompany them.

Copymaster 30 (In our school)
This copymaster should be used to collect words and ideas for a poem describing lots of different things going on in the school. The children go round the school and record on the copymaster a list of things they'd like to put in their poem, made up of sounds they can hear, things they can see and things that people are doing.

The children should then work on each idea to make a list poem. You may want to read them this example:

In our school we heard –
children chattering while they worked,
pots and pans clattering in the canteen,
the school clock tick tock.

In our school we saw –
a photo of a blue whale deep beneath the sea,
a painting of yellow flowers,
a velvet curtain.

In our school we saw –
crows pecking in the playground,
Mrs Bancroft listening to children read,
the little ones dancing to music.

Copymaster 31 (Standing on my head)

This copymaster shows an upside-down poem! The children can use the phrase 'I am standing on my head' and repeat this, adding in reasons why they may be standing on their head. They could invent different linking phrases, such as 'I am hanging upside down'. Let the children do their rough draft on a separate sheet, using the copymaster to write down the final version. The following example could be used as an illustration of what is needed.

I am standing on my head
so that I can see the world from an ant's point of view.

I am standing on my head
so I can hold up the world.

I am standing on my head
because my new trainers are hurting.

I am standing on my head
in case I swallow my tongue.

I am standing on my head
so that I don't tread on any beetles.

I am standing on my head
so my trousers don't fall down.

I am standing on my head
because I was tired of standing on my own two feet.

Copymaster 32 (Menu poem)

This poem uses the format of a menu. Before writing on the copymaster the children should make notes and produce a first draft of a menu poem. This should be redrafted and proofread before it is copied out neatly on to the menu sheet. The children will need to decide for what occasion their menu will be used – a monster's party, a menu for making the teacher happy, a menu for making Dad mad? Below is an example which you could show children to give them an idea of what is wanted here.

Menu for making my teacher angry

First course
A delicious pâté made of squabbling children served on slices of warmly toasted spelling mistakes.

Main course
A well-roasted class fight in a sauce of rude jokes sprinkled with giggles.
This is served with mashed bad handwriting, boiled moans and groans and grilled pinchings.

Pudding
Straight from the freezer, an ice cream of fighting topped with a swirl of punches.

Copymaster 33 (The secret box)

Let children stick enlarged copies of the copymaster on to card and cut out the box template. On to each inside cover children should write a special secret. You may want to read aloud this list to stimulate the children:

Five secrets
1 My dad is Superman.
2 I keep a star inside my pillow.
3 A lamppost spoke to me this morning.
4 My cat can take his skin off.
5 I ate a slice of sunlight.

Before making the box the children should draw careful designs on the outside that have something to do with the contents. Children can then glue the flaps and fold the template together to make the box. When it is complete the secrets will be trapped on the inside – it will be a 'secret box'.

The children could write a poem about their secret box, saying where they found it, what it is made of and what it might contain. Ralph (nine years old) wrote the following:

I found my box
trapped in the centre of a star.
Its sides are made of
bees' wings and pollen.
Its lid is carved from
the rough tongue of a dragon.
Its hinges are made of
the jaw bones of a crocodile
I saw bathing in the sun's furnace.
If you press your ear
to the sides of the box
you would hear the buzz
of many insects.
My box contains
the secret of the wind's invisibility.

Copymaster 34 (Dragon's eggs)

Enlarge this copymaster before distribution. The dragon shown here has laid eggs. Each egg contains a baby dragon that has different feelings – get the children to think of a list of possible feelings (sad, lonely, hungry, angry, jealous, etc.). Under each egg the children write one of these feelings; inside the egg they write down how their dragon will behave. So, an egg that is labelled 'angry' could have 'crushes villages in a spurt of fury' written inside it . An egg labelled 'sad' could contain 'curls up and cries tears of gold'.

Copymaster 35 (Jumbled poem)

The lines and words of this poem have become quite jumbled up in my computer. The children should cut up

4

the lines and try to reconstruct the poem, adding any extra words that are needed.

The following is my version. The children will create many different variations; as long as the poems make sense they are valid, though some, of course, may read more effectively than others.

Owl

Owl
was darker
than ebony –
flew through the night,
eyes like amber searchlights,
rested on a post,
feathers wind-ruffled,
stood stump still,
talons ready to seize
and squeeze.

Owl
was death
for it flew through the dark
that swamped the fields,
that tightened its knot,
that bandaged the hills
in a blindfold of fear.

Owl flew – Who – Who – Who –

Copymaster 36 (Spider calligram)
Using the faint outline of the spider the children write their chosen sentences on the spider's legs so that the words make the drawing. I have done one leg. Before writing on the copymaster they should make a list of useful words, phrases and ideas. These may be written as sentences or just as words.

Copymaster 37 ('Odd Kettle of Fish')
This poem consists of everyday phrases that have had their meanings taken literally. Once children have read the poem, they should spend several days collecting sayings and phrases of their own. These should then be displayed on the wall and the children can try writing their own poems. *Brewer's Dictionary of Phrase and Fable* (Cassell) is a useful source of sayings. Here are some to start your list:

laugh your head off/like a hyena
slam the door in your face
silence is golden
look a gift horse in the mouth
it's raining cats and dogs
as quiet as mice
over the moon.

Copymaster 38 (Animal riddle acrostic)
The riddle on the top half of the page is an acrostic, with the key word, 'Badger', hidden in the centre of the poem

in bolder print. On the lower part of the copymaster the children should begin their own acrostic by writing the subject of their poem – an animal – down the centre. Each line is then built on either side of one of the letters that spell out this animal.

Copymaster 39 (Open door)
The children should colour each door in a different colour in faint pencil crayon. The children should make a list of things that are the same colour as the doors. There should be a yellow one, blue one, green one, red one and so on. Then they write the first draft of a poem for each coloured door on a separate piece of paper, redraft this and proofread it, before copying it neatly on to the doors on the copymaster. So, for a blue door, children may write:

Beyond the blue door
are skies that stretch,
seas that roll by,
a flash of the kingfisher,
stripes on a parrot fish,
school jumpers
and a sad moment.

Joanna (eight years old) wrote on her red door:

My red door
is blood from a cut,
Tanya's hair,
a streaky sunset,
our school jumpers,
when Dad is angry,
building bricks
and post office vans.

Copymaster 40 (School rap)
Use this copymaster as a worksheet to carry on with the school rap I have begun. The children could work alone or in pairs. They should insert the school's name into the space provided and continue the rap on the copymaster. As they write, they should try to maintain the same rhythm. The teacher may need to try out several with the whole class. To help with the rhythm the children will need to say the rap aloud to 'hear' if it sounds right. Raps can be presented as performance pieces with percussive background. Children will need time to prepare and practise their raps. To write other raps use a simple format such as:

Hip hop hap
it's the football rap

or

Hop hip hap
it's the disco kid rap.

FURTHER IDEAS

Stories
Use postcards of paintings or posters to start a story. Seaside and holiday images tend not to work well –

however, people, scenes, events and places can be used successfully. Lay the postcards out and let the children choose one which appeals to them. This can then become the front cover for a story they are about to write or be an illustration in the story itself. I have found that some of the Surrealists' pictures, in particular, intrigue children.

Use music to start a story or poetry writing. Select a piece that you feel may be atmospheric or exciting and get the children to listen. They can start writing as they listen or afterwards.

Dress up a child in a costume and get the other children to decide who the child might be, what they are like, where they come from and what has happened. This information may then be woven into a story. Alternatively, the teacher could determine some of the information about the character and start telling the children a story with the character in it.

Bringing in objects. Use an object to start a story. For instance, bring a mirror into class and tell the children that it is a magic mirror which, if you gaze into it, can enable you to see into the future. You could also use keys, boxes, rings, a ship in a bottle and other intriguing items. Suggest a few ideas to get the children going, for example 'What does this key unlock?', 'What secret is held inside this box?', 'If you put this ring on what might happen?'

Writing 'on location'. Most writing takes place inside the classroom. For a change, take the children out – to a church, a park, an old cinema, the playground – and use this as a starting place for a story. What happens, who comes along? I have had successful writing from visiting churches, a turkey farm, an old house and a hay field.

Retelling a tale but changing one aspect. A useful way into this idea might be to read one of the many children's stories based on traditional tales such as *Clever Polly and the Stupid Wolf* by Catherine Storr. In such stories a traditional tale has been taken and parts of it altered – a princess becomes a boy, or a wolf becomes gentle. The children will need to take a tale they know well and alter a character, the setting, some of the events or the ending.

Inventing a huge lie. In a way all stories are huge lies, so making up lies itself can lead into stories. For instance, you could tell the children that you came to school on an elephant this morning and it is parked at the back of the school. Ask the children to invent a similar 'whopper' and, having invented the lie, consider what might follow as a consequence.

Stories about what happens when children swop places for the day with their mum, dad, brother, sister, best friend or teacher.

Tape-recording stories. Instead of children writing let them use a tape-recorder to tell their stories; the finished version should be played back to the class. Some children will wish to retell the stories having heard their first version.

Telling a story in a circle. Put the children into a circle.

The first person begins a story – 'Once upon a time there was a girl called Jane' for example – and each child takes it in turn to add the next sentence. This activity can be great fun.

Drawing a story before or instead of writing. This can be done as a cartoon or as a single illustration. It is suitable for very small children who cannot write or for much older children who struggle with composition.

Stories based on books read. For example having read *Mrs Pepperpot* children imagine they are small.

Stories about discovering a magic ring or key. What power does it have? What might happen?

Let the class know several days in advance that you want them to write a story and ask them to 'find' one. The children may want to ask parents, neighbours, friends or grandparents. The story could be true or a traditional tale.

Leaving a secret message on the class newsboard – for example you may leave a message which says 'HELP! I AM TRAPPED, signed Laura'. This message should be used by the children as the start to a story. The children should consider where they found the message, who it is from and what happens.

Putting a storyteller's hat in the bookcorner. Whenever you read or tell a story put on the hat. Leave it for the children to try.

Stories about giants or fierce monsters that need defeating.

Telling a story with a contrast – sad clown, happy ogre, frightened lion, giggly dragon and so on.

Making a sign: 'DO NOT ENTER', 'DO NOT TOUCH'. Where is it, why is it there, what happens if you ignore it?

Stories about being trapped or in a cave.

Stories about being lost.

Useful first lines

- The door creaked open and Sally sat up in bed.
- The egg had definitely begun to crack open.
- John picked up the stone. It glowed in his palm.
- The trees in the forest sighed. The King had died and his only daughter was to be Queen.
- In the land of Gooder there is a place where you can see into the future. If you dare. When Kim stared into the future pool she saw ...
- He hadn't meant to steal but ...

Poems
Collecting playground rhymes.

Secrets – 'It's a secret but
       my Dad is Superman.'

Dreams – 'I dreamed I was ...'

Would you rather – 'Would you rather be a funny person
have a new bike or …'

Magic Box – 'In my magic box
I would have
a burning sun
the moon melting …'

Flying – 'If I had wings I could feel …
If I had wings I could see …
If I had wings I could touch …
If I had wings I could be …'

What you are – finding different ways of comparing parts of the body.

'Your head is like a round football.
Your eyes are blue as the sky.
Your nose is like a white pear …'

Weather – the rain, snow, storms, wind and hot sun are all potent stimuli for writing.

People – describing unusual people.

Places – describing special and secret places. Looking at the landscape, taking notes on the roadside. Listing things that are happening:

'A man drives home in his Peugeot,
dice dangling in the rear window.
A new grandmother waits at the bus stop,
a baby's shawl in her bag …'

Without you – listing things that might happen if someone left:

'Without you peanuts would loose their crunch,
my brain would turn to mud,
ants would rule the world …'

Don't worry – 'Don't worry if the world floods with rain,
if windows start to cry,
if Superman turns into Donald Duck …'

I want – listing impossible and real wants:

'I want to touch
a blaze of lightning.
I want to write a dream
that never ends.
I want to destroy
the evil in people's hearts …'

You make me feel – this idea is a chance to use rhyme. It comes from a poem by Adrian Henri, as does the 'Don't worry' idea listed above.

'You make me feel like a coyote's thumb
You make me feel like Big Daddy's tum.
You make me feel like a pound of cheese.
You make me feel like a plate of peas.'

Counting rhyme – 'One, two, three, four
Monsters knocking at my door …'

Riddles – getting the children to focus on a subject and jot down a list of its attributes: the things they know and notice about it. The secret of a riddle, remind them, is to give a list of clues without giving away what the subject is.

Sounds – describing noises. Imagine it is night-time. The children hear a noise. What could it be?

'Who is there?
Is it the midnight fox
searching the dustbins?'

Alphabet poems – A ate an apple, B bit a banana, C caught a carrot and so on. The poems could be about food or an event, for instance a visit to the sea:

'A arrived on the beach.
B built a sandcastle.
C caught a crab.
D dug a pit.
E …'

Seasons poem. Under a heading for each season the children write a list of all the seasonal events they can think of. For example:

'In winter –
The snow smothers the trees,
icicles hang like frozen fingers,
bright lights sparkle in shop windows,
tinsel decorates the Christmas tree,
carols are sung on the telly …'

Night poem. Brainstorm a list of words and ideas to describe the sights, sounds and events of night-time. Read Abdul's poem as an example:

At night
the shadows slither
down dark streets.
The lights in the flats
shine like a ship.
People queue at the chip shop.
Cars sneak by.
Their bonnets shine
like polished shoes.
Behind the curtains
TV mumbles on.

Teaching tips
● Before the children write, read out one or two examples – preferably by other children.
● When writing a poem that uses a repeating phrase, such as 'without you …', always do one or two lines with the whole class so they understand what you want.
● End sessions by hearing some of the children's work read aloud.
● With younger children use a flip chart and transcribe for the group. You should do this often.

Shopping tale

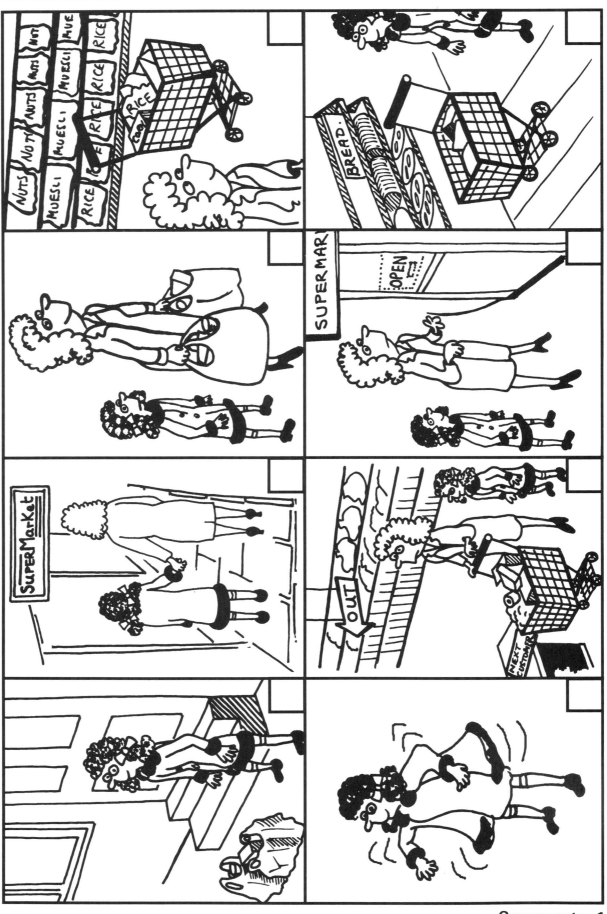

Starters

'Come back,' shouted the old man.

Once upon a time there was a beautiful woman who lived all alone in the middle of a forest.

I woke up and could hear something scratching at the door.

On our way to school this morning we found a golden ring.

There was a giant who lived near our village and he had a terrible temper.

We were late for school but when we got there we found that ...

Copymaster 2

? ✒ ? ✒ Story questions ? ✒ ? ✒

What title could you give your story? Try out several possible titles.

What are the names of the main people in your story?

Where does the story take place?

What time of day is it?

What is the weather like?

How does the story begin? Try out your first line here.

Copymaster 3

Supposing stories

Supposing you woke up and found that you had become really small …

Supposing you turned into a cat or a dog …

Supposing you could make yourself invisible …

Supposing your best friend turned into a monster …

Copymaster 4

Story builders

Characters

Places

Events

Copymaster 5

12

Fairy tale headlines

 FAIRY TALE TIMES

Princess catches thieves

Wolf is defeated

Prince finds treasure

Trolls found in woods

Copymaster 6

Endings

So, the children ran out of the cave into the sunshine. They still held the old man's bag. They sat down on the sand to see what might be inside.

The unicorn said goodbye and spread its wings to fly home.

Miss Fussy said that she would never teach Class 2 again.

Jo said she was sorry to Mum and this time she meant it.

Sam lay down on her bed.

It was great to be home.

'I'll never tell another lie.'

The fox sniffed the wind and knew that spring would soon arrive.

Copymaster 7

The magic box

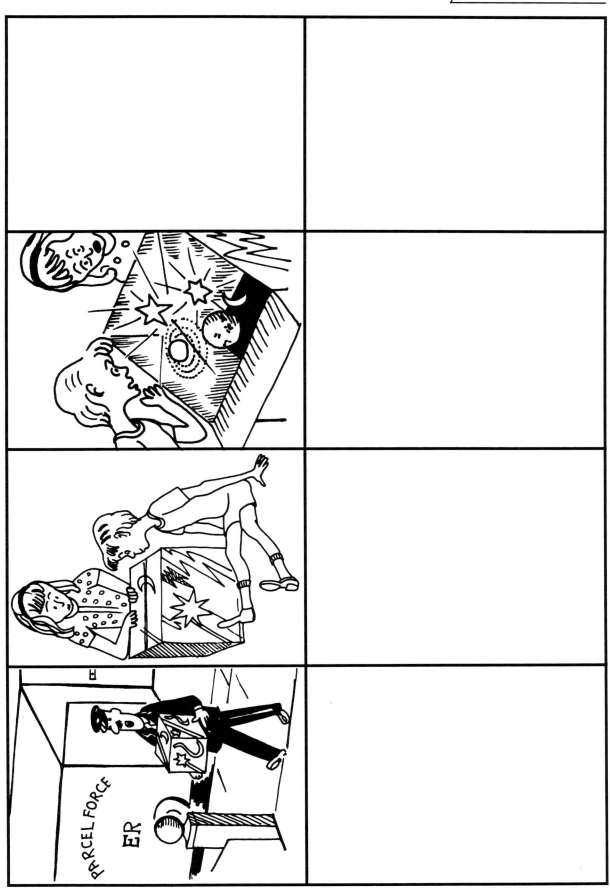

Trolls

When the sun set it was dark in the forest. Soon the animals were fast asleep. Only the trolls were awake. They were busy building a boat.

All night long they fetched wood and banged nails. When the morning came they took their new boat down to the river. Now they would be able to cross it.

Octopus story

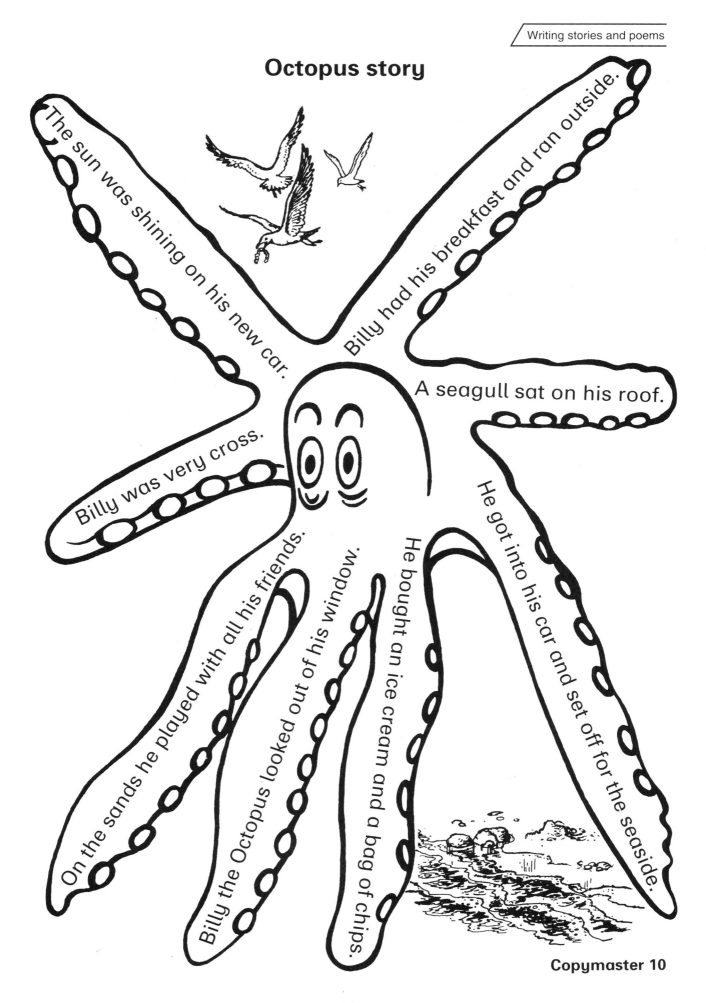

The sun was shining on his new car.

Billy had his breakfast and ran outside.

A seagull sat on his roof.

Billy was very cross.

He got into his car and set off for the seaside.

On the sands he played with all his friends.

Billy the Octopus looked out of his window.

He bought an ice cream and a bag of chips.

Copymaster 10

Story flow chart

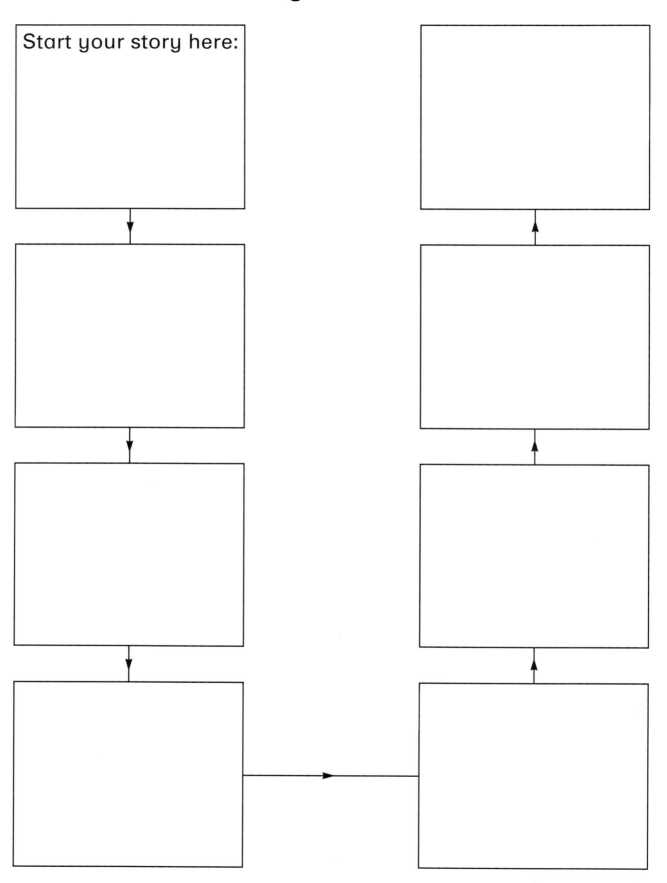

Start your story here:

Expedition 1

3 kg	2 kg	1 kg
1 kg	$\frac{1}{2}$ kg	$\frac{1}{2}$ kg
$\frac{1}{2}$ kg	$\frac{1}{2}$ kg	3 kg
4 kg	1 kg	$\frac{1}{2}$ kg
4 kg	2 kg	$\frac{1}{2}$ kg

Copymaster 12

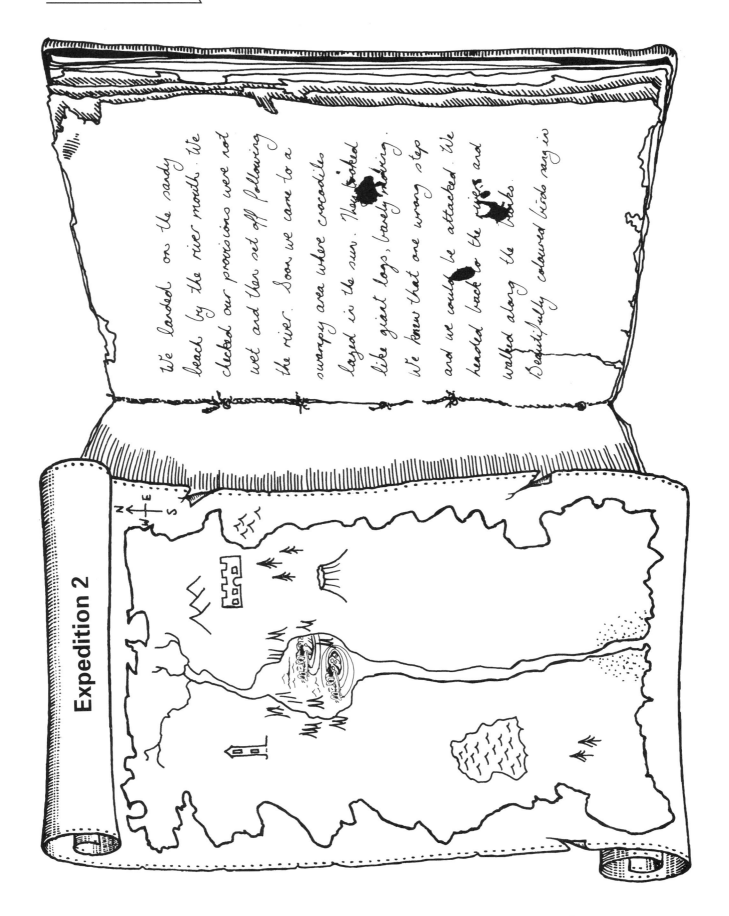

We landed on the sandy
beach by the river mouth. We
checked our provisions were not
wet and then set off following
the river. Soon we came to a
swampy area where crocodiles
lazed in the sun. They looked
like giant logs, barely moving.
We knew that one wrong step
and we could be attacked. We
headed back to the river and
walked along the banks.
Beautifully coloured birds sang in

Expedition 2

Messages

If you know
good for
meet me
midn

Help! I am
stranded on
Boot 9oland.

Don't speak to the
man at the sweetshop.
I know where the
money is hidden.

found the
outside door
and you
night you

LOST AT SEA.
NO FOOD OR
WATER.
LAST
SEEN NEAR

Bare bones

1 There was a girl and a boy who went on holiday by the sea. They built a dragon out of sand. That night the girl went down to the beach and the dragon came alive. She took it home and hid it. It layed eggs. The eggs hatched into lots of sand dragons. The woman in the house where they were staying was very tidy. She got cross with the children because there was sand everywhere. So the children tried hiding the sand dragons …

2 There was a girl who was always in trouble at school. One day she drew a pair of glasses on a poster of Henry the Eighth. Her class teacher caught her doing it. She made her stand outside the headteacher's door. While she was standing there she saw someone stealing money from the head's room and sneaking out of a window. She ran after them …

3 The Queen had a daughter who never smiled, so she said that whoever made her daughter smile could have as much treasure as they could carry away. So lots of people came to the castle to try to make the girl laugh. They told jokes, they told funny stories, they did silly dances, they played tricks. But she did not laugh. Until one day a poor boy came to the palace. He had a parrot with him …

Copymaster 15

Potion stories

Copymaster 16

Magic wishes

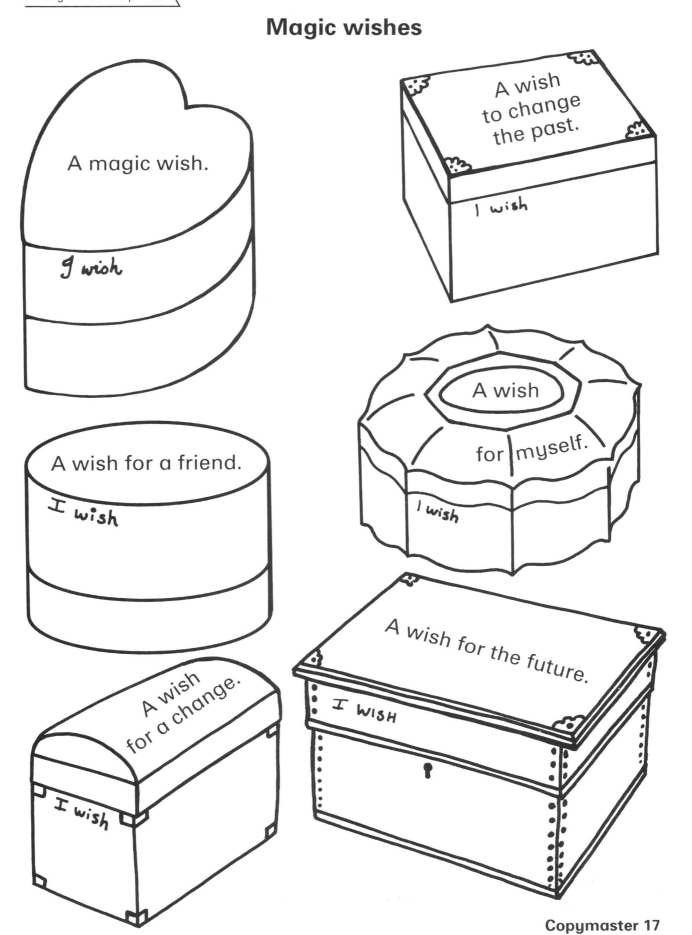

A magic wish.

I wish

A wish to change the past.

I wish

A wish for a friend.

I wish

A wish for myself.

I wish

A wish for a change.

I wish

A wish for the future.

I WISH

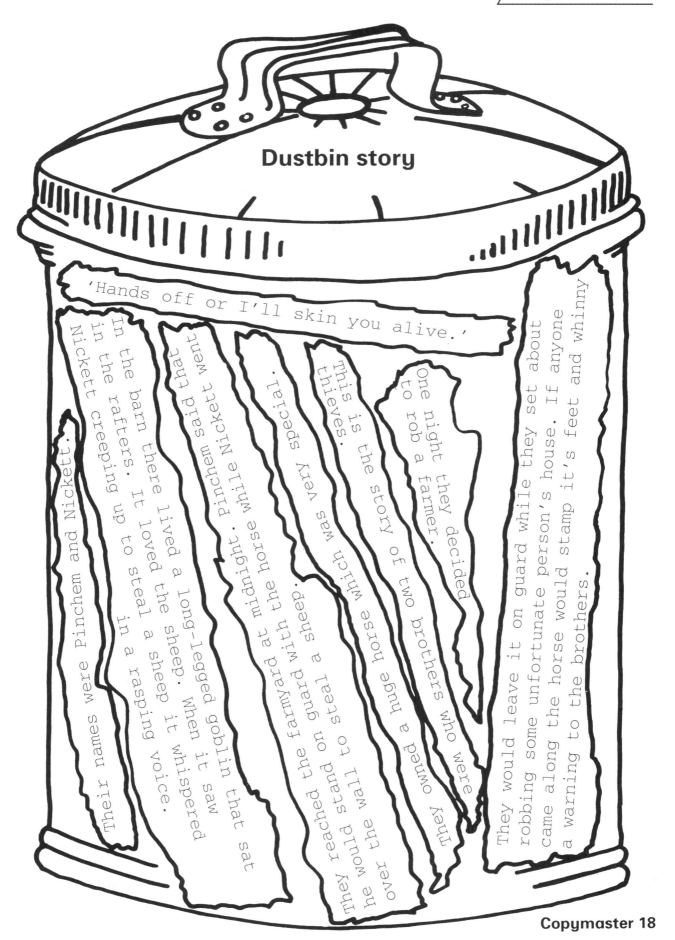

Dustbin story

'Hands off or I'll skin you alive.'

Their names were Pinchem and Nickett.

In the barn there lived a long-legged goblin that sat in the rafters. It loved the sheep. When it saw Nickett creeping up to steal a sheep it whispered in a rasping voice.

Pinchem went while Pinchem went while midnight. horse at the farmyard with the sheep.

This is the story of two brothers who were very special.

They reached the farmyard and stand on guard to steal a sheep. They would stand on guard to steal a huge horse which was wall to over the

One night they decided to rob a farmer.

They owned a huge horse which was very special.

They would leave it on guard while they set about robbing some unfortunate person's house. If anyone came along the horse would stamp it's feet and whinny a warning to the brothers.

Copymaster 18

Story skeleton

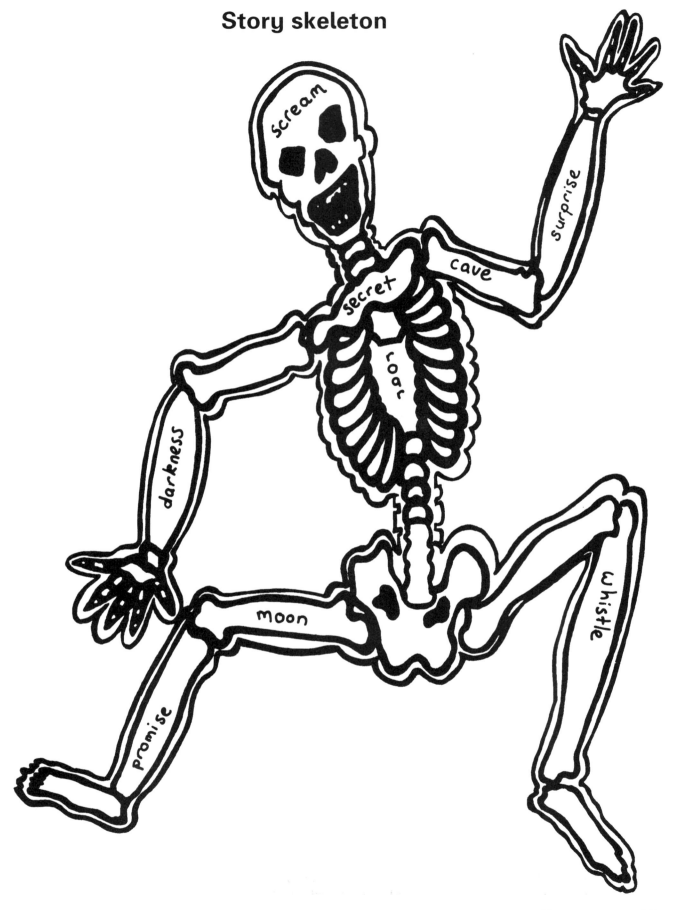

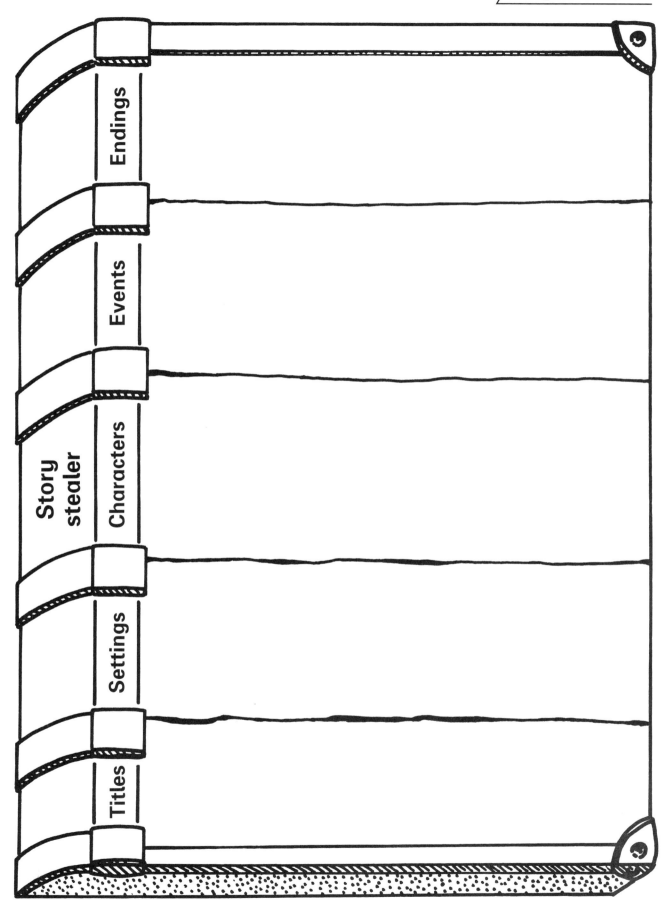

Story stealer

Endings

Events

Characters

Settings

Titles

Rainbow poem

Key

- red
- orange
- yellow
- green
- blue
- indigo
- violet

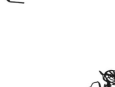

Counting poem

One	One white whale went for a sail.
Two	Two tiny trees sat on their knees.
Three	Three thirsty thieves collected leaves.
Four	Four fat frogs sat on logs.
Five	Five funny foxes sat in boxes.
Six	Six silly sweets started to tweet.
Seven	Seven silent sausages started to scream.
Eight	Eight late plates opened up the gate.
Nine	Nine naughty newts dressed up in suits.
Ten	Ten tired toads crossed the road.

Copymaster 22

29

Place I'm in:

Listen

What is making the noise?

Words to describe the sound

I am afraid

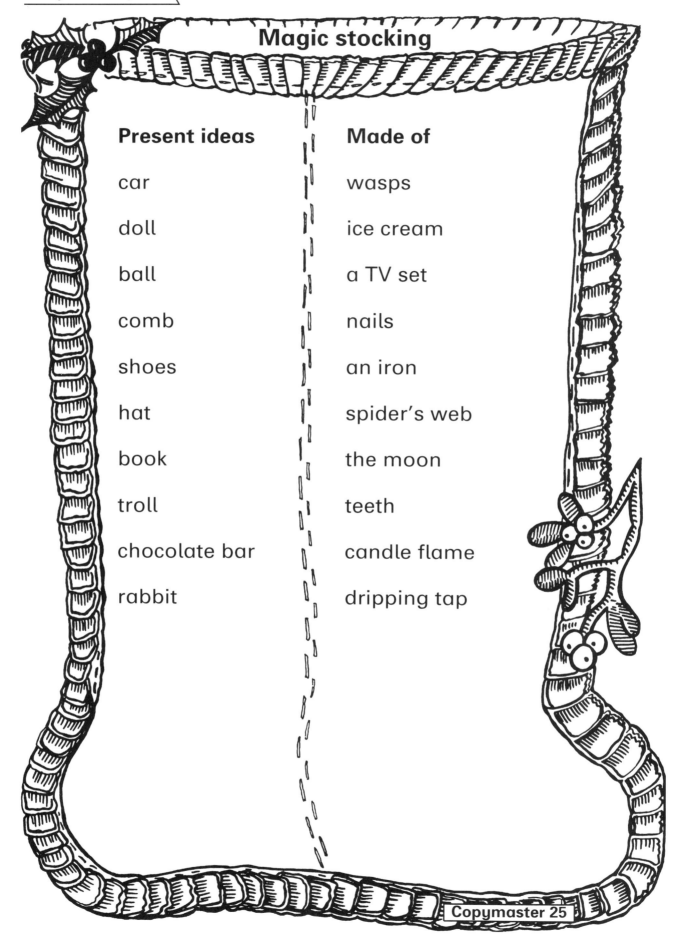

Magic stocking

Present ideas	Made of
car	wasps
doll	ice cream
ball	a TV set
comb	nails
shoes	an iron
hat	spider's web
book	the moon
troll	teeth
chocolate bar	candle flame
rabbit	dripping tap

Copymaster 25

Crazy wishes

I wish I was a mouse
scuttling for safety.

I wish I could fly
over the roof tops.

I wish ...

Copymaster 26

33

Sea word-picture

Bonfire calligram

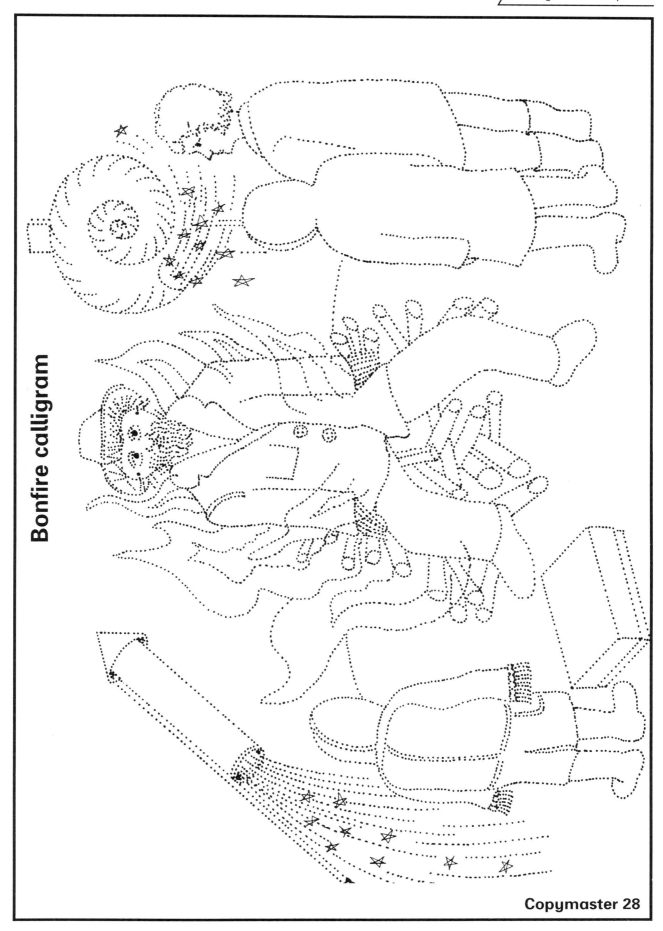

Copymaster 28

Animal poem

Imagine a snake
thin as a …

_____

Imagine a cat

_____

Imagine a pig

_____

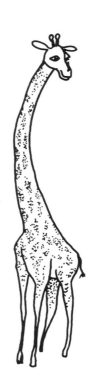

Imagine a dog

_____

Imagine a flea

_____

Imagine a giraffe

_____

Imagine a bear

_____

Imagine a seal

_____

Copymaster 29

36

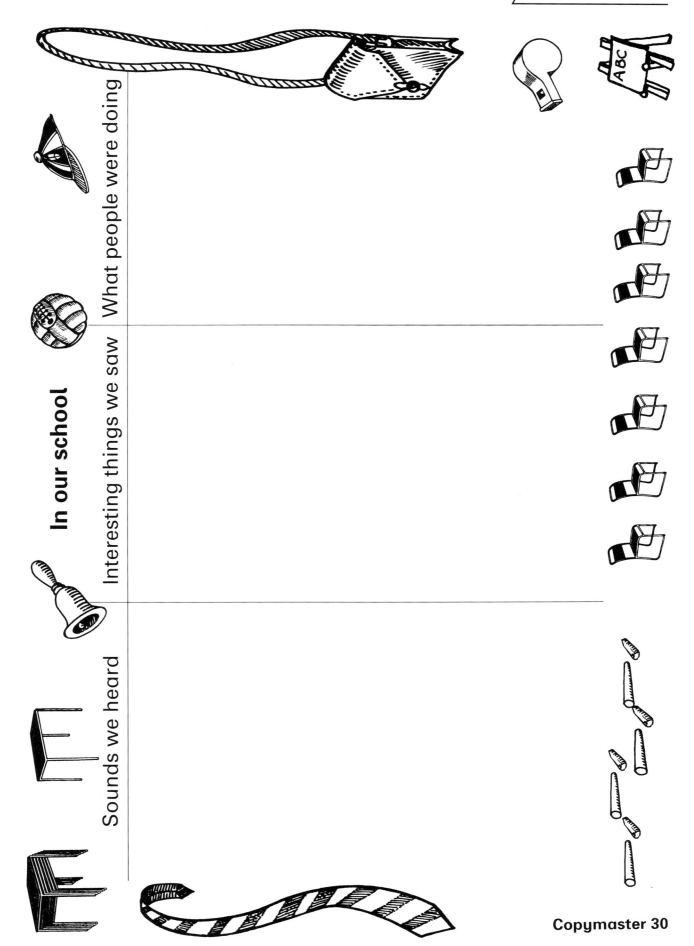

In our school

What people were doing

Interesting things we saw

Sounds we heard

Copymaster 30

Standing on my head

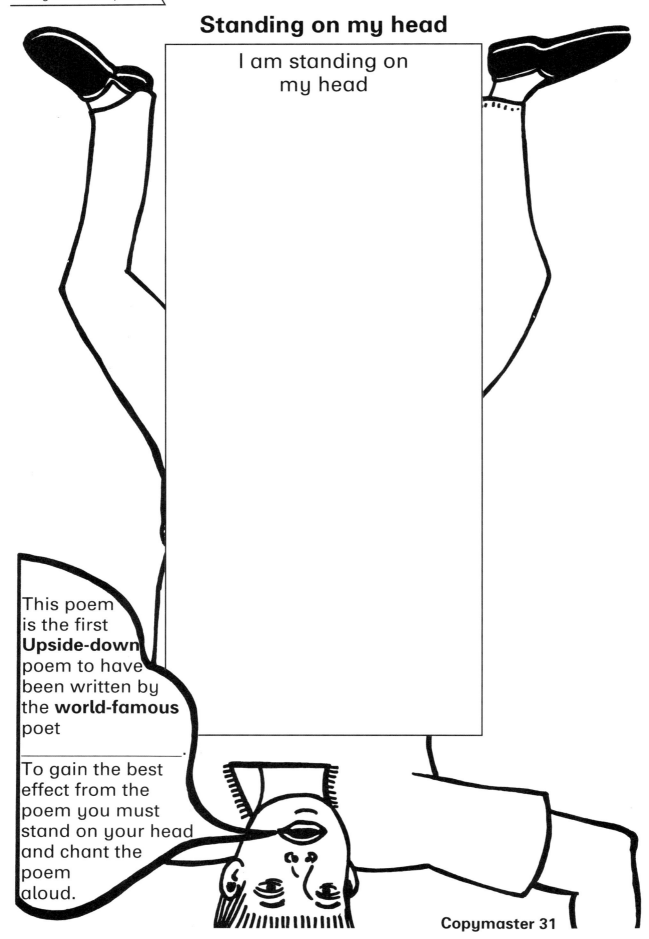

I am standing on
my head

This poem
is the first
Upside-down
poem to have
been written by
the **world-famous**
poet

_____

To gain the best
effect from the
poem you must
stand on your head
and chant the
poem
aloud.

Copymaster 31

  **Menu poem**

A menu for_____

 First course

 *Main course*

 Pudding

Copymaster 32

The secret box

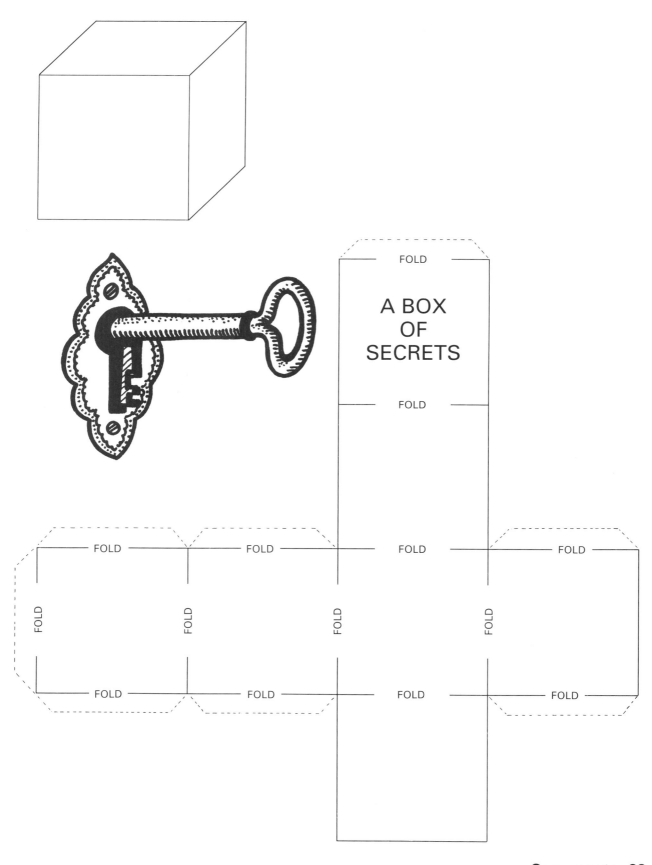

A BOX
OF
SECRETS

FOLD

FOLD

FOLD

FOLD

FOLD

FOLD

FOLD

FOLD

FOLD

FOLD

FOLD

FOLD

FOLD

FOLD

Copymaster 33

40

Dragon's eggs

Jumbled poem

was death

was darker

that bandaged the hills

eyes like amber searchlights,

Owl

than ebony –

rested on a post,

in a blindfold of fear.

that swamped the fields,

flew through the night,

and squeeze.

OWL

that tightened its knot,

Owl

for it flew through the dark

feathers wind-ruffled,

Owl flew – Who – Who – Who –

talons ready to seize

stood stump still,

Copymaster 35

Spider calligram

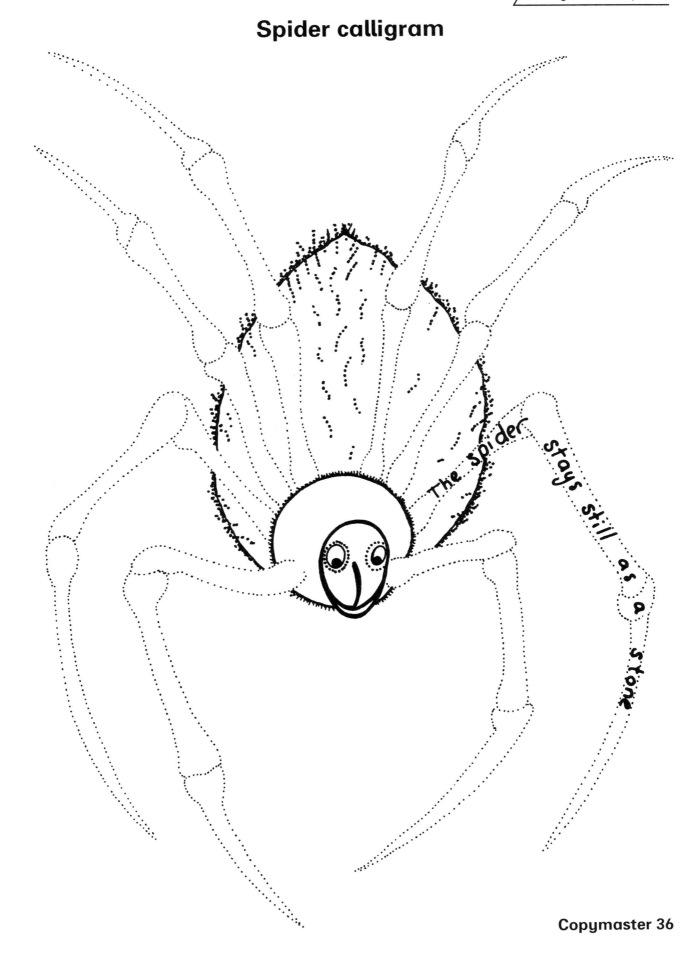

The spider stays still as a stone

'Odd Kettle of Fish'

1 The detectives said that
The books had been cooked.
(They tasted good.)

2 My teacher said we could
have a free hand.
(I added it to my collection.)

3 Some people bottle up
their feelings.
(I keep mine in a jar.)

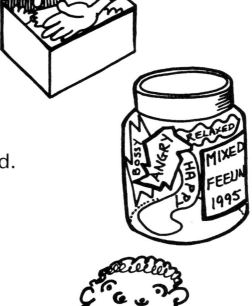

4 My mother said –
'Hold your tongue!'
(It was too slippery.)

5 When my sister laughs
she drives me round the bend.
(I catch the bus back.)

6 Dad told me
to keep a stiff upper lip.
(It's in a box by my bed.)

7 My uncle is a terrible
name dropper.
(I help my aunt
to sweep them up.)

8 In the school races
I licked everyone in the class.
(It made my tongue sore.)

Copymaster 37

44

Animal riddle acrostic

Like a small **B**ear

    bundles over the dark road.

Brushes p**A**st the front gate,

    as if she owns the joint.

Rolls the **D**ustbin,

    like an expert barrel rider.

Tucks into yesterday's **G**arbage,

    crunches worms for titbits.

Wak**E**s us from deep sleep,

    blinks back at torchlight.

Our midnight feaste**R**,

    ghost-friend, moon-lit, zebra bear.

Open door

Copymaster 39

School rap

Hip hop hap
it's the _____ school rap

We like to do our very best,
we hardly like to take a rest.

Hip hop hap
it's the _____ school rap

Our teachers call us funny names,
we like it best when we play games.

Hip hop hap
it's the _____ school rap

Copymaster 40

WRITING FOR INFORMATION

This section introduces writing in a range of different forms – recipes, captions, greetings cards, letters, news items, signs, lists, instructions, adverts and information. Consideration is given to ensuring that children think about the audience and purpose and how these affect the form, content and layout. Some copymasters require children to think about sequencing and to change text to make it easier for a certain audience to read. The particular demands of different forms of information writing are highlighted through children using the copymasters in this section, sharing what they have written and critically considering each other's approaches. Children are introduced to the notion of using headings and to terms such as 'glossary' and 'contents'.

Copymaster 41 (My life list)
Down one side of the copymaster is a list of facts about the life of a girl called Daisy. The children have to select some facts from their own lives and complete the second column. This could be extended by children adding on other pieces of information about themselves, through either writing or drawing. Older children could design their own 'passports'.

Copymaster 42 (Muddled recipe)
The children need to look carefully at the pictures and then read the recipe statements below each picture. These have been muddled up. The children could cut out and reassemble the recipe, sticking the finished piece on to a clean sheet. This activity could lead on to writing or drawing recipes when doing classroom cooking. It introduces the idea of the term 'recipe' and leads into the activity on Copymaster 43.

Copymaster 43 (Funny recipe)
This recipe copymaster is an invitation to make a recipe for creating a new person. The children should read the recipe poem in pairs. They then decide what sort of person they would like to make and should list the ingredients, look in a recipe book and list the sorts of words and phrases used in recipes, for example 'take a pinch of, add a slice of, stir, let this simmer, place in a hot oven' and so on. The recipe should be written in the space provided on the copymaster. This could then be cut out and mounted. A class book of recipes could then be made.

Copymaster 44 (Captions)
This copymaster requires the children to look carefully at the pictures. For each picture they have to write a caption to describe what is happening.

Copymaster 45 (Invitations)
The children have to read the top half of the copymaster which is an invitation to a monster's party. They can then decide on the sort of party they themselves would like to hold. The bottom half of the copymaster is for the children to complete their own party invitation.

Copymaster 46 (Fairy tale postbag)
Read aloud with the children the two letters from the fairy tale characters. The children should then write a reply to each one.

Copymaster 47 (*Golden Goose Chronicle*)
Get the children to reply to this letter which appeared in the fairy tale newspaper. There is space on the copymaster for a reply, or a separate piece of paper could be used.

Copymaster 48 (Street signs)
This copymaster shows a street scene with various blank signs and notices. The children need to discuss what the signs might be for and choose their words carefully to fill them in.

Copymaster 49 (Animal lists)
This is a simple activity where the children have to draw a line from the animal to the adjective which best describes it. The children can only make one choice, so they will have to consider which word they think is best. Beside each animal they should then write a sentence on the line provided using the words, for instance 'The cool cat purred'.

Copymaster 50 (Picture news)
On this copymaster the children have to write or tell the news item that goes with each picture.

Copymaster 51 (Draw it)
This is the reverse of the above activity. Here the children have to draw the illustration that goes with the news. They need to read carefully in order to draw what has been written about. Drawings could be compared and discussed.

Copymaster 52 (Instructions)
The picture shows two children arguing over a game. Nearby is a skipping rope, a ball and a hopscotch game. The children decide on their favourite playground game and in the space provided write the rules for playing it. The completed copymasters should be swopped around so others can read the rules and see if they are clear enough for them to play the game.

Copymaster 53 (Spot the bias)
This copymaster invites the children to read the newspaper article and spot the bias in the writing, namely that the journalist obviously favours one football team over another. In pairs the children should read the article carefully and underline any word or phrase that they think is biased. This should be followed by a rewrite of the news report in the space on the copymaster or on a separate piece of paper in one of two ways: a) biased in favour of the other team;   b) in as fair a way as possible.

Copymaster 54 (Book recommendation)
This copymaster can be used for children to complete after reading a book they have enjoyed. It is intended that they should record information on this sheet that would be useful to others looking for a good read. The copymaster should go into a folder kept by the library entitled 'Recommended reads'.

Copymaster 55 (Adverts)
On this 'noticeboard' there are a number of blank 'for sale' signs so that the children can advertise friends, teachers, characters from books and so on. One is filled in as an example.

Copymaster 56 (Layout)
This copymaster contains some basic information about China that needs to be set out better. The children can draw lines on the sheet to indicate where they would break the text into paragraphs, and add a title for each section in the margin. Alternatively, the children can cut up the text into sections, pasting them on to a fresh sheet underneath the titles they have thought up. This information should then be rewritten with pictures for a different audience – younger children, another class, as a letter for a friend or as a holiday brochure.

Copymaster 57 (Rewrite)
The piece of information on this copymaster has been written for older children. The task here is to produce a simplified information sheet for a class of seven- or eight-year-olds. The children should underline pieces that will need changing. They need to think of titles for different sections and decide which parts will need illustrating. Finished versions should then be compared and given to younger children to see if they can enjoy the new text!

Copymaster 58 (Information list)
Sally has been looking in reference books and has made a list of facts that she has found out. At the moment the information is muddled up – the children should work on the list, organising the facts into groups. The information can then be written up as interestingly as possible as a fact sheet.

Copymaster 59 (Computer error 1)
The computer has made a terrible mistake with printing out this letter. The children have to cut the letter up and reassemble it so that it makes sense.

Following is one of the possible versions the children might end up with – though other variations may make good sense as well.

```
Wildlife Safari Park,
Kimpton,
Sussex.

Dear Joanna,
I am writing to thank you for your recent
letter. I am pleased that you enjoyed your
visit to the Wildlife Safari Park.

You are right to point out that we do run
a conservation programme. We aim to
rehabilitate animals. It is our aim to use
the park to ensure that endangered species
can survive. We also hope to educate the
public. If it is fun as well then that is
an extra bonus.

Once again I am pleased that you arrived
home safely from your visit and thank you
for your kind words.

Yours sincerely,
Jane Carter.
```

Copymaster 60 (Headings)
This activity is about making a fact sheet for your own school. The child on the copymaster has begun by thinking of some headings to write about. The children have to sort the headings shown into a sensible order. Some headings should be dropped if they aren't appropriate. The children should then use their study skills to discover more about each heading and write a fact sheet for the school.

Copymaster 61 (50-word items)
The challenge of this copymaster is that the editor of the newspaper shown has only got two 50-word spaces left. The children should write on the copymaster in the spaces provided in 50 words or less. The class could then be divided into editorial groups. The 50-word stories should be read aloud and voted on for interest and clarity. Groups should vote to see which are the best-written stories and justify their choices.

To extend the activity, children could invent their own headlines and swop them over with a partner, before writing another 50-word news report.

Copymaster 62 (Glossary and contents)
Down the left-hand side of the copymaster is a list of words from a glossary. The children should complete the space provided by writing down what the words mean. Reference books (e.g. *The Aztecs* by R. Nicholson and C. Watts, Two-Can, 1991) may be needed here! The right-hand side lists the contents. In the space provided the children should write down what subjects they would expect each item to cover. This could be followed by the children being given a book title such as 'The Greeks' (or a title relevant to a topic the children have just covered). They should then produce a glossary and a contents list for a reference book on this subject. This will give you some insight into what was learned from the topic!

49

FURTHER IDEAS

A newsboard – children can write at home and pin things up in class.

A class scrapbook for children's home writing or to publish 'best' pieces.

Drawing or painting 'news' items.

A class diary – a different child to write in it every day.

Writing letters to other classes inviting them to watch a class show or presentation related to work that is underway, or a short play or a reading of poems or stories.

Writing letters to the headteacher thanking him or her for visiting the class show.

Writing letters organising a school/class outing and thanking those who helped or who have been visited afterwards.

Writing thank you letters to parents and helpers who listen to children reading.

Writing letters to local newspapers/radio stations. These might be about special events or activities in school or relate to local events or concerns. For instance, a Cardiff primary school wrote to the local waterboard complaining about pollution in a nearby river. They were invited to watch the council pull a car out of the river!

Writing letters to authors whose work has been enjoyed – these might contain questions as well as comments on the author's writing.

Using *The Jolly Postman* by Janet and John Ahlberg to generate fun letters based around traditional tales. For example, Lucy wrote a letter to the big, bad wolf:

```
Dear Mr Wolf,

I am concerned that you have been seen
hanging around the park recently. My
sister and I often play on the swings and
we do not wish to be eaten up. If you
carry on with your bad ways we will have
to send for the local wolf-catcher and you
will be put in a home for bad wolves.

Yours sincerely,

Lucy, nine years old.
```

Designing a boardgame and writing instructions for it.

Writing instructions for classroom needs – e.g. keeping the bookcorner tidy, feeding the class gerbil etc.

Writing lists of what children know before doing a topic.

Writing lists of what children have learned after a topic.

Writing captions to go with displays and pictures. Captions could be in the form of statements or questions.

Putting labels on displays, belongings and equipment. Children become used to labelling items indicating who they belong to or what they are for.

Writing invitations for class and school events.

Writing greetings cards for key festivals and special occasions.

Making posters concerned with school rules – e.g. 'Please walk, don't run' etc.

Using writing to plan, jot down and order ideas. Demonstrate this in front of the children.

Persuasive writing – writing opinions and arguments. Show children how to organise the pros and cons.

Describing people – friends, relatives, old people, unusual people, special people.

Describing places – local places, holiday resorts, seaside places, towns, villages, woods, secret hiding places, markets, libraries, churches, cinemas, funfairs etc.

Describing events – at the doctor's, the school fête, the school concert, a wedding, sports day, going greyhound racing etc.

Using different types of books as models for children to learn from. Let them read part of Roald Dahl's autobiography *Boy* and then write up some incidents from their own life.

Writing a 'Did you know' book related to a particular topic. Every child could contribute a number of pages, each one beginning with the words 'Did you know ...?' The rest of the page is about an interesting fact to do with the project.

Writing an 'Is it true?' book. Each child can contribute two sides. On the first side the children write a fact followed by the words 'Is it true?' Over the page is the answer plus an illustration and perhaps one more interesting fact. For example, from an 'Is it true?' booklet on birds:

Humming birds got their name because they can hum tunes. Is it true?	No, but they can hover like a helicopter

Making a simple pamphlet about the topic in hand – this may mean writing an information booklet for a younger class about the area being studied. Children should consider how the needs of the younger audience will affect the writing and presentation.

Writing an information poster or fact sheet. In pairs the children select a topic and write a series of questions they would like to find the answers to. They use reference books to discover the answers and present this information on a poster or small fact sheet. These could be displayed on the wall or duplicated for each class member. For example, one class wrote a series of fact sheets on outer space – one sheet for each planet.

My life list

Daisy's life list

I was born in 1989.

My birthday is in April.

My hair is fair.

My eyes are blue.

I am 98 centimetres tall.

My favourite colour is blue.

My favourite food is bacon.

I live in a cottage.

I have a cat called Choco.

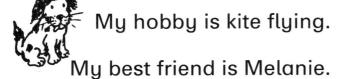

My hobby is kite flying.

My best friend is Melanie.

Your life list

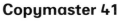

Copymaster 41

51

Muddled recipe

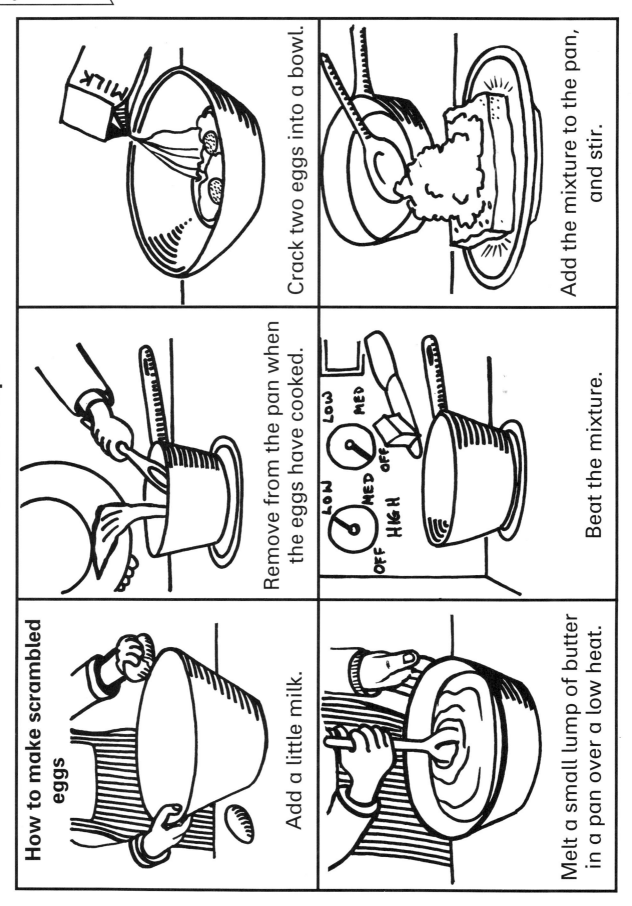

Crack two eggs into a bowl.

Add the mixture to the pan, and stir.

Remove from the pan when the eggs have cooked.

Beat the mixture.

How to make scrambled eggs

Add a little milk.

Melt a small lump of butter in a pan over a low heat.

  **Funny recipe**

RECIPE

This person is made of baked tuna and brown rice.

Her hair is made of boiled spaghetti hoops
and slices of cucumber.

Now add in a hamburger for her face.

To make eyes stir in pickled onions.

Let this simmer with carrots for a nose.

Place in a hot oven.

RECIPE

This person is made of ...

Copymaster 43

53

Captions

Copymaster 44

Invitations

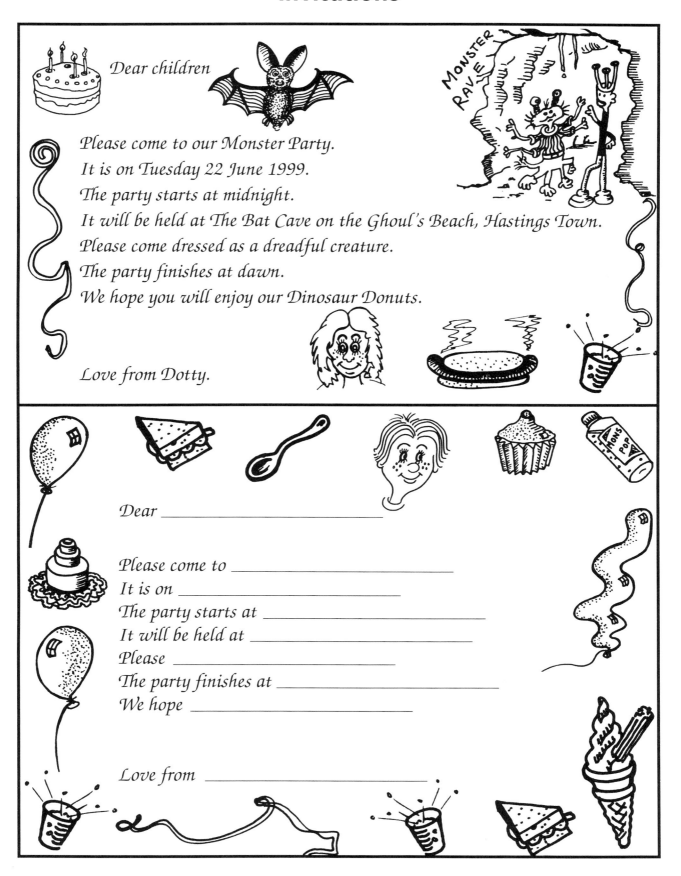

Dear children

Please come to our Monster Party.
It is on Tuesday 22 June 1999.
The party starts at midnight.
It will be held at The Bat Cave on the Ghoul's Beach, Hastings Town.
Please come dressed as a dreadful creature.
The party finishes at dawn.
We hope you will enjoy our Dinosaur Donuts.

Love from Dotty.

Dear _____

Please come to _____
It is on _____
The party starts at _____
It will be held at _____
Please _____
The party finishes at _____
We hope _____

Love from _____

Fairy tale postbag

Dear Wolf,

We are all fed up with you chasing us around. You have blown 2 of our houses down. We are scared of going out in case you eat us up. Why can't you be friendly or take a long holiday in Australia?

Love,
the little pigs

Dear Hansel and Gretel,

I am sorry that you ran away from my lovely little house made of sweets. I cannot think why you did not want to stay.

I am baking a lovely pie to eat and wondered if you would like to come and see me soon.

Love from,
the kind old lady
xxx

Copymaster 46

Golden Goose Chronicle

Price 6 p.

Dear Sir,

I am writing to complain about the theft of two magic pots which I had hidden in my kitchen. One of my pots was called 'Plenty' and if you asked it to cook, it would boil you up a pot of porridge. My other pot was very special. If you put one thing in you would pull out two of the same! If anyone has seen these pots please let me know,
Yours sincerely,
Jack the Piper's cousin.

Reader's reply:

Copymaster 47

Street signs

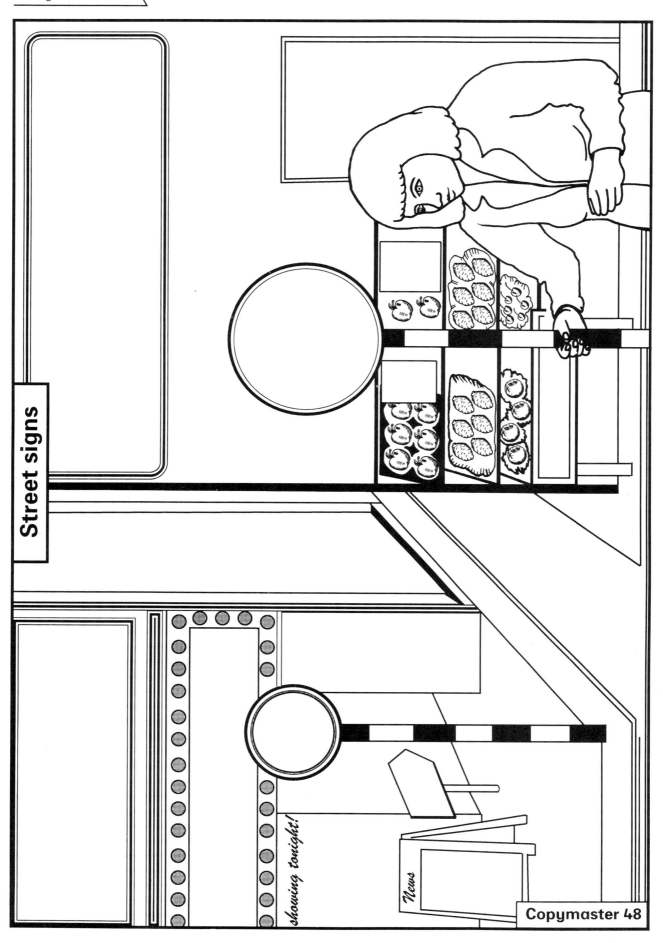

showing tonight!

News

Copymaster 48

Animal lists

Animal	Description	Write a sentence
cat	tiny	_____
dog	cool	_____
bear	furry	_____
zebra	cuddly	_____
snake	fierce	_____
tortoise	shaggy	_____
monkey	slithery	_____
tiger	slow	_____
porpoise	stripy	_____
ant	bouncy	_____

Copymaster 49

Picture news

LION AT LARGE!

_____
_____
_____
_____

SCHOOL CROC SHOCK!

_____
_____
_____
_____

Draw it

PRINCESS PRESENTS PRIZES

On Friday afternoon two children from Ethelbriggs Road School won a painting competition. The children had to paint a picture of their favourite animal. The Princess of Wales presented the prizes of £10 each to the winners. They were Lucy Luck and Ron Deering, both aged seven years old. The prizes were presented in the local gardens where the Princess also saw the roses and flowers in bloom. She enjoyed an ice cream and saw the ducks at the boating pond. Afterwards the children said it was great to meet a real princess.

Instructions

Rules for playing _____

Spot the bias

ROVERS – TEAM OF THE MATCH

Last night Rovers played against Wolves. From the beginning Rovers played superbly despite losing four unlucky goals. Their striker, Dunne, was unfortunate to be sent off when he made an excellent tackle. Throughout the game Rovers found themselves defending against Wolves and were beaten by some lucky strikes. Johnson, playing with the wind in the wrong direction, defended his goal at all times against the attackers. The Wolves' attackers got away with an off-side which the referee missed. Rovers tackled well despite several warnings and managed to shoot at goal no less than ten times. There were a number of lightning shots by the Rovers' attackers which only missed because of the wind direction.

Copymaster 53

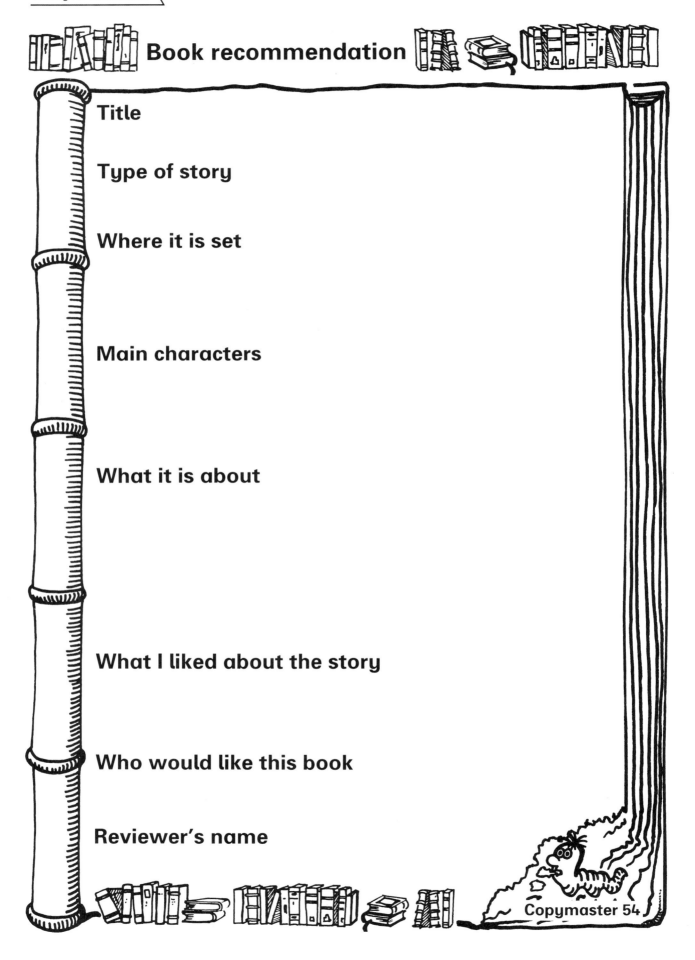

Book recommendation

Title

Type of story

Where it is set

Main characters

What it is about

What I liked about the story

Who would like this book

Reviewer's name

Copymaster 54

Adverts

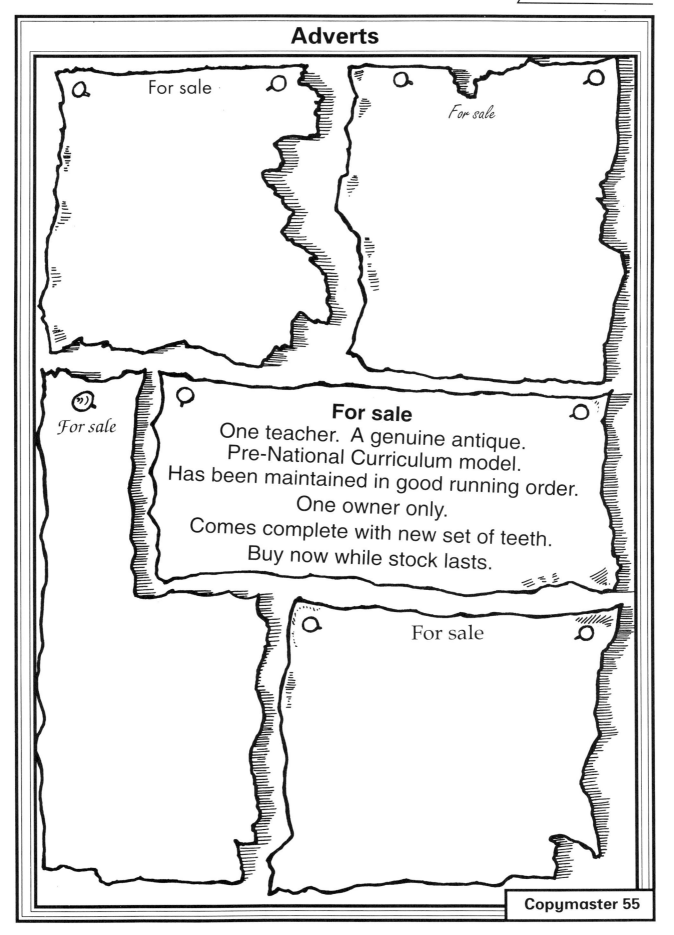

For sale

For sale

For sale

For sale
One teacher. A genuine antique.
Pre-National Curriculum model.
Has been maintained in good running order.
One owner only.
Comes complete with new set of teeth.
Buy now while stock lasts.

For sale

Layout

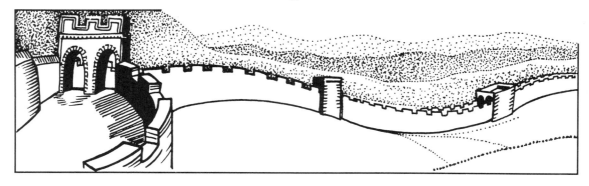

China is a large country. It reaches for more than 3000 kilometres. There are mountains, forests, deserts and tropical areas. The Great Wall of China was built to keep out invaders. At one time 30 000 men were working on the Wall. It is between 5 and 10 metres high. You can walk along the top of the wall. There are watch-towers along the wall. It was originally 6000 kilometres long. The Chinese believed that the Wall was really a dragon that had fallen asleep. The Chinese invented a number of different things that we still use today. They made gunpowder and used this to create the first fireworks. They also invented a strange-looking wheelbarrow. This was called the wooden ox. They floated magnets on bowls of water to act as compasses. They built giant water-clocks that rang out every quarter of an hour. Rich people in China ate a wide variety of foods. The poor people ate mainly vegetables, millet, rice, noodles and bread. They ate with chopsticks. The rich drank rice wine while the poor drank green tea.

Copymaster 56

Rewrite

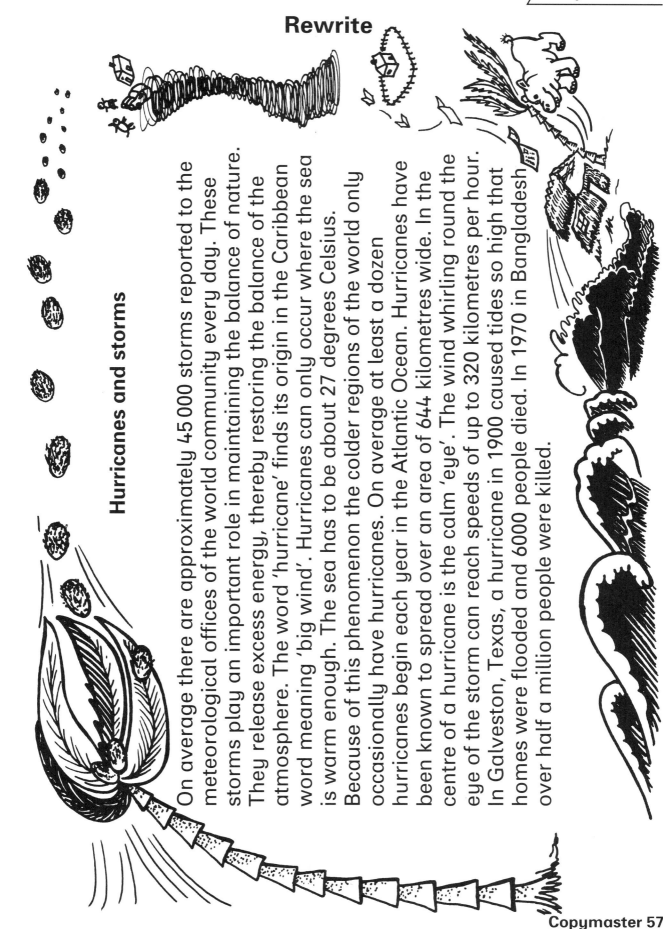

Hurricanes and storms

On average there are approximately 45 000 storms reported to the meteorological offices of the world community every day. These storms play an important role in maintaining the balance of nature. They release excess energy, thereby restoring the balance of the atmosphere. The word 'hurricane' finds its origin in the Caribbean word meaning 'big wind'. Hurricanes can only occur where the sea is warm enough. The sea has to be about 27 degrees Celsius. Because of this phenomenon the colder regions of the world only occasionally have hurricanes. On average at least a dozen hurricanes begin each year in the Atlantic Ocean. Hurricanes have been known to spread over an area of 644 kilometres wide. In the centre of a hurricane is the calm 'eye'. The wind whirling round the eye of the storm can reach speeds of up to 320 kilometres per hour. In Galveston, Texas, a hurricane in 1900 caused tides so high that homes were flooded and 6000 people died. In 1970 in Bangladesh over half a million people were killed.

Copymaster 57

Information list

Ancient Egypt

In 5 000 BC farmers grew crops on the banks of the Nile.

They believed in life after death.

From 2 700 BC they built pyramids.

The pyramid at Saqqara was 62 metres high.

They mummified bodies to preserve them.

Villages and towns were ruled by kings called pharaohs.

In 2 450 BC the Great Pyramid of King Khufu was built.

They were buried with their possessions.

It took over 2 million bricks to build the Great Pyramid.

Pyramids were tombs for the pharaohs.

The Great Pyramid was 147 metres high.

Copymaster 58

Computer error 1

Wildlife Safari Park,
Kimpton,
Sussex.

the public.

and thank you for your kind words.

It is our aim to use the park

can survive.

I am pleased that you arrived

Yours sincerely,

You are right to point out that

to ensure that endangered species

If it is fun as well

I am writing to thank you

I am pleased that you enjoyed your visit

to the Wildlife Safari Park.

Dear Joanna,

we do run a conservation programme.

We aim to rehabilitate animals.

for your recent letter.

Jane Carter.

We also hope to educate

home safely from your visit

Once again

then that is an extra bonus.

Copymaster 59

69

Headings

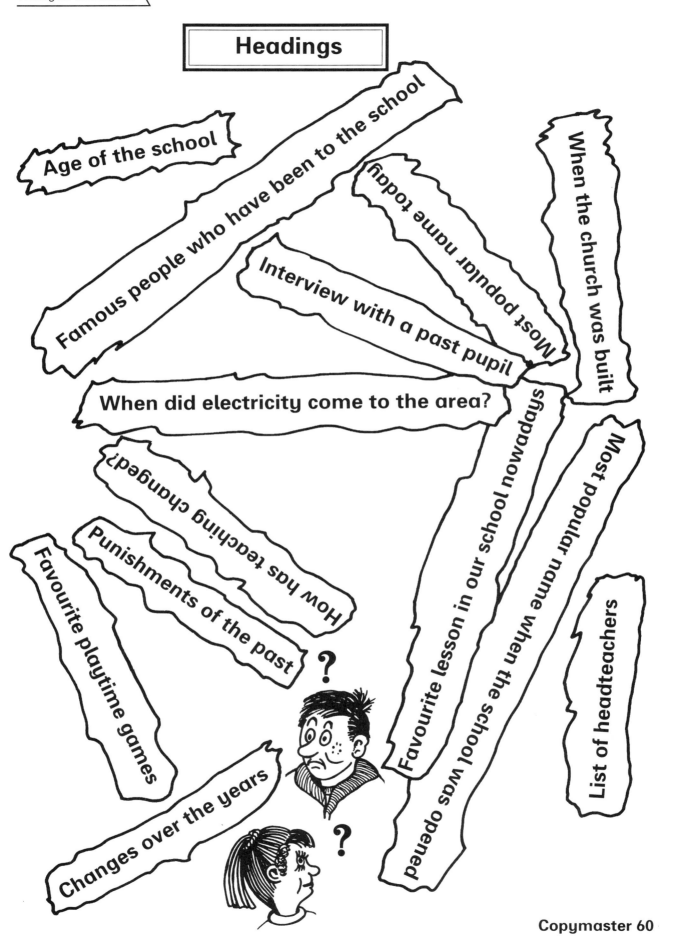

Age of the school

Famous people who have been to the school

Most popular name today

When the church was built

Interview with a past pupil

When did electricity come to the area?

Most popular name nowadays

Most popular name when the school was opened

How has teaching changed?

Punishments of the past

Favourite playtime games

Favourite lesson in our school nowadays

List of headteachers

Changes over the years

Copymaster 60

50-word items

STORM HITS SCHOOL

DOG FINDS TREASURE

Glossary and contents

Glossary

Contents

Calpolli

Chinampas

Codices

Maguey plant

Pulque

Tlazcalli

The Aztec people

Aztec worship

Crafts

Farming

Clothing

The Spanish

Food

Copymaster 62

72

WRITING FROM READING

This section focuses upon one important aspect of writing: that all writers develop through the influence of what they have read. Children are shown the importance of learning how to write from their reading – to find out how writers gain their effects by reading as a writer. Some of the copymasters require children to **imitate or emulate** a certain style or approach, while others require the children to **respond** to a piece of writing, sometimes jotting down ideas, thoughts and feelings, and at other times writing in various forms – letters, diary entries or stories.

Copymaster 63 (The playground)
Children should tell the story of what is happening in the picture. By talking or writing they could respond to specific questions: How does the teacher on duty feel? What has she seen happening? What is she thinking about? Pick on different incidents in the picture for the children to consider – they could give names to some of the children and then consider what they may be doing, who their friends are, why they are behaving in this way, what they are feeling and thinking, what they may be saying and what will happen next.

Copymaster 64 ('The White Bear')
There are a range of activities that could arise from this story. Children could circle all the wintry words and make a collection that could be added to. They could discuss why the man wanted to take the bear to the King and what the King might do when they arrived. The children could cut the story into sections, sticking them on to separate sheets of paper and then illustrating to make a simple book. The children could then continue by completing the story.

Copymaster 65 ('C Poem')
This poem should be carefully read aloud by the teacher. Children could then draw each item in the poem on the copymaster. They may then wish to choose other letters – I and O are easy ones to start with – and make a list of things that these letters are similar to. This could then be made into a list poem. For instance:

O is a mouth singing,
a party balloon in the sky,
the sun in the summer,
a two-penny piece,
one of Dad's juggling balls,
the steering wheel on our car,
a beefburger,
the middle of an egg …

Copymaster 66 ('In the Cold')
Again this poem could be illustrated, this time with drawings of the different animals. The children could write down how the poem makes them feel and what it makes them think of. This could then lead into children writing their own poems in imitation of the simple forms 'In the sun', 'In the rain', 'In the snow', 'In the wind', 'By the sea' and so on. For instance:

In the sun –
cows sleep by hedges.

In the sun –
sunbathers lie on their towels.

Copymaster 67 ('The Wise Man and the Tyrant')
This story is a good one to tell. The children should reread the copymaster and then begin by drawing the sequence of events as a cartoon. This will help them to visualise the story. The children should then try retelling the tale in pairs, helping each other. They should then practise in a larger circle, taking it in turns. This could be followed by children telling the story in pairs to children from another class. Other possible response activities include:

• Writing the diary of the faithful servant, describing the day when his master almost lost his head
• Writing a letter from someone in the crowd to a relative about what they saw
• Writing the story of what happened to the faithful servant next, continuing the tale from the copymaster
• Writing a list poem in which children imagine they have become the wealthiest person alive, listing what they would spend their money on. Joanne wrote:

If I were so wealthy I would –
feed the people of Somalia
till their tummies were like drums,
save the whale by buying the ocean
and declaring it a whale-safe zone,
build houses for the people
who live in cardboard boxes,
buy up all the zoos in the world
and rebuild them so that the animals
had plenty of space to roam in …

Copymaster 68 ('The Growler')
This is a true story. Children could jot down their initial responses – any thoughts, feelings or things they are reminded of. These could then be shared and discussed. Key questions to discuss may be: Why did the teacher do this? How did the little boy feel? What would the other children have thought? Writing in response could take

as its subject the boy telling his mum what had happened, the teacher telling another teacher, or the children pretending they were in the class and writing an account of the scene from their own viewpoint.

Copymaster 69 ('City Jungle')
Read the poem aloud carefully. The children should jot down their initial impressions and thoughts – how they felt, what it reminded them of. They should underline parts they did and did not like and bits that puzzled them. These should be compared and discussed. The children should underline or circle words that make the different objects sound like creatures. They should draw a picture showing some of the parts of the scene described. Their circled pictures and words should be compared. The children should then choose a place to write about – seaside, forest, river, village, estate, arcade, cinema, market, supermarket, station, etc. – and list the key objects they wish to put into the poem. They should then work at each object, using imagery to make them sound like something else – animals, birds, insects, fish, flowers, fruit, trees, plants, feelings, vegetables, etc. For instance:

> The sea crawls
> on its hands and knees
> spitting out stones.
>
> Rocks squat
> like toads waiting.
>
> Seaweed waves its hair.
> The wind clenches
> its icy teeth.

> The beach-huts stare
> as solemn as monks
> at the streak of horizon.
>
> Towels blossom,
> beachballs bloom.
>
> The waves chatter
> to themselves.

Copymaster 70 ('Wind Poem')
This poem was written after one of the great storms of the 1980s. The children should read the poem carefully and then jot down and discuss what picture the poem makes them imagine. The children should circle all the words that are powerful and that make the wind sound strong, and then underline all the rhymes and half-rhymes. Children should then compare what they have decided to underline/circle. This will give rise to fruitful discussion as to why certain words have been chosen or not. The children should then choose an aspect of the weather to write about, imitating the style of the poem yet choosing a set of words that are appropriate to the subject. So for a sun poem, hot words will be needed. For instance:

> Sun blisters the earth.
>
> The turf curls up,
> dry as toast.
>
> Sun withers flowers,
> showers evaporate.

FURTHER IDEAS

Jotting down the first impressions and reactions to stories, poems, TV and radio programmes.

Writing notes about what you did and did not like, what puzzled you (what you do not quite understand, what questions you have or what you are curious about) and what patterns/connections you noticed? These four areas – likes, dislikes, puzzles and patterns – are fruitful topics for discussion and comparison. It is useful to encourage children to discuss the parts of stories and poems that puzzle them and talk their way towards deepening their understanding.

Writing a letter to a character in a story giving advice.

Making a family tree to show the characters in a story.

Drawing the picture that stays in children's heads after they've read a poem.

Drawing a map of the story.

Designing a front cover.

Reading a poem and guessing the (previously unseen) title.

Stopping at a key moment in a story and writing the thoughts that might be running through the main character's head. This key moment could be from the 'class novel' that the teacher is reading and could be a group or individual reading task. An example of a suitable key moment is in *The Hobbit*, when Bilbo is lost in the darkness and can hear Gollum. What thoughts might be running through his mind?

Drawing a time line to show the sequence of events in a story.

Writing a news report of events from a story or poem.

Jotting down feelings about a poem, character, place or event. Children should think about what the writing made them feel and what memories it stirred.

Keeping a diary for the main character in a book such as *The Hobbit*.

Writing an estate agent's brochure to sell a place from a story.

Writing an end-of-term report for the main character at the end of the story.

Making brief notes and discussing what changed in the story.

Interviewing a character from the story.

Cutting up a poem and letting the children reassemble it.

Commenting on a character or incident – 'How I see Gandalf' or 'What I think about …'

The playground

'The White Bear'

Once upon a time there was a man who had a white bear. Now this bear was so beautiful that the man decided he would take it to see the King.

When they set off it was summer and the sun warmed them on their way.

Soon it became autumn and the leaves fell from the trees.

Then it was winter and the snow fell thick and fast.

On Christmas Eve they came to a cottage in the woods. They were very cold and very hungry. They had not eaten for three days.

The snow crunched beneath their feet. It covered the trees. Its icy breath blew into their faces. They looked like white ghosts drifting through the forest.

So they knocked at the door of the cottage hoping for shelter.

Copymaster 64

77

'C Poem'

A cup, a chin,
the silver moon,
a bridge, a nose,
tip of a spoon.

A grin, a snail,
a shrimping net,
a giant's ear,
a snakey pet.

A monkey's smile
a finger nail,
a pirate's sword,
a fisherman's sail.

Copymaster 65

'In the Cold'

In the cold –
the badger hides in her set.

In the cold –
the robin fluffs out her feathers.

In the cold –
the dormouse curls into a ball.

In the cold –
the fox lies snug in his den.

In the cold –
the squirrel sleeps in her drey.

In the cold –
our cat creeps up to the fire.

In the cold –
we dress up warm and wish for the sun.

Copymaster 66

'The Wise Man and the Tyrant'

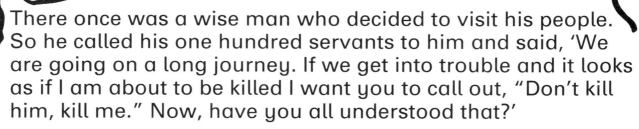

There once was a wise man who decided to visit his people. So he called his one hundred servants to him and said, 'We are going on a long journey. If we get into trouble and it looks as if I am about to be killed I want you to call out, "Don't kill him, kill me." Now, have you all understood that?'

His one faithful servant that was left behind said, 'Yes, oh Master.' So it was that the two of them visited many towns and villages till in the end they came to the main square of a city where the cruellest tyrant in the world lived. And the cruel tyrant was in a terrible temper.

'What are you looking at?' shouted the tyrant at the wise man. 'Oh, nothing' replied the wise man.
'I'm not "nothing". I'm a great King,' roared the tyrant. 'Off with his head.'

Soon a crowd had gathered to see the wise man have his head cut off. Just as the axe man was about to do his duty the faithful servant remembered what he had to say and shouted out, 'Don't kill him, kill me.' The tyrant was amazed and had the servant dragged to him. 'Why do you wish to be killed instead of this man?' asked the tyrant.

'I'm sorry,' said the wise man, 'but he has heard of the prophecy that states that on this very day, in this very place, the man who has his head chopped off will live for ever and become the richest and most powerful man in the world.

'Richest and most powerful!' shouted the tyrant. 'Live for ever!'

So it was that the cruellest tyrant in the world lay down his own head on the chopping block ...

Copymaster 67

'The Growler'

When I was about five years old I had a teacher called Miss Woolett. She was tall and had very long golden hair. She had it piled up on her head and some of it hung down in ringlets. She was very pretty.

One afternoon we were standing round the piano singing when she stopped playing and looked at us.

'Now then, one of you is making a horrible growling noise,' she said. 'Which one of you is spoiling our song?'

I looked round to see who the culprit might be. When I looked back she was staring at me.

'Now, don't you sing anymore. Just open and close your mouth but I don't want to hear any sound come out at all.'

That afternoon I felt like a goldfish.

Copymaster 68

'City Jungle'

Rain splinters town.

Lizard cars cruise by;
their radiators grin.

Thin headlights stare –
shop doorways keep
their mouths shut.

At the roadside
hunched houses cough.

Newspapers shuffle by,
hands in their pockets.
The gutter gargles.

A motorbike snarls;
Dustbins flinch.

Streetlights bare
their yellow teeth.
The motorway's cat-black tongue
lashes across
the glistening back
of the tarmac night.

Copymaster 69

82

'Wind Poem'

Wind slices its icy blade.

Wind raids trees,
smacks leaves up back streets.

Wind somersaults sheets,
bustles and kicks.

Wind flexes muscles,
flicks its quivering wrist.

Wind twists dustbins
into clattering cartwheels.

Wind curls its steel tongue
like a shout flung at the sky.

Wind sighs;
Dies.

Copymaster 70

83

WRITING FROM PERSONAL EXPERIENCE

This brief section is concerned with ensuring that children's personal writing, formed directly from their own home experience, is not forgotten. Whilst many infant children are familiar with talking about their weekend 'news' on a Monday morning, this use of personal experience often dies out in the junior years. The copymasters in this section focus on the use of memory and explore the diary format.

Copymaster 71 (Memory time line 0–7 years)
Into each box the children draw a key memory. The copymaster can then be cut up and the drawings used as headings to pieces of writing that describe the memories. If they aren't yet old enough, the children could draw something they are looking forward to in the box. While children have no memory of years 0–2/3, they may well have gained second-hand knowledge about incidents that happened at this time, for example moving house or a baby brother being born. Children could fill in the copymaster with someone at home.

Copymaster 72 (Memory boxes)
This time the boxes have headings. The children draw a relevant memory into each box. What happened can be told to the teacher or a group, or the boxes can be cut up and used as illustrations to a written account.

Copymaster 73 (My diary)
Here the children use the questions to help them write an account of what happened yesterday.

Copymaster 74 (Memory time line 7–11 years)
This time line provides for key events for junior-age children. The children draw into each box a key memory from that age. The copymaster can be cut up and a 'Memory Poster' made, using the boxes as illustrations to written accounts about each memory. As before, children who aren't old enough can draw what they are looking forward to in coming years.

Copymaster 75 (Memory jogger)
Under each heading the children jot down any words or ideas that come with the relevant memory. It may help them if they close their eyes and try to 'see' the memory. Get the children to share their lists with a partner and to tell the story of some of their memories. This can then lead on to children circling the memory with the most potential for writing and submitting a written piece for inclusion in a book of class memories.

Copymaster 76 (Gnome's diary)
This copymaster shows a few pages from a gnome's diary. Using very small writing the children should try to complete the blank diary pages on the copymaster. They may wish to cut out the four diary spreads, sew them in the middle with one stitch (see Copymaster 84) and make a miniature book.

FURTHER IDEAS

'The funniest thing that has ever happened to me.'

'The saddest time I had.'

'A family row.'

'When I went to hospital/was ill.'

'My biggest fear is …'

'The best holiday we had …'

'The most important event in my life.'

'When Mum/Dad/Gran/Teacher got angry.'

'A time I cried.'

'What I do after school.'

'A new person in the family.'

'A pet we had.'

'Moving home.'

'First day at school.'

'Memories of the infants' school.'

'What I am looking forward to ...'

'What I am not looking forward to ...'

'A part of my work I find hard ...'

'Parts of my work that I enjoy ...'

'Personal Writing' books – these are private journals. The pieces of writing can be marked with a capital P which means they are private and will be read only by the teacher (not aloud to the class). The children are allowed to write on any subject they wish.

Memory time line
0–7 years

1 year old	**2 years old**	**3 years old**	**4 years old**

5 years old	**6 years old**	**7 years old**

Copymaster 71

Memory boxes

Best holiday

A funny time

A sad time

When I was angry

In trouble

Copymaster 72

  **My diary**

1	2	3	4	5	6	7
8	9	10	11	12	13	14
15	16	17	18	19	20	21
22	23	24	25	26	27	28
29	30	31

What was yesterday's date?

When did you get up that morning?

What did you have for breakfast?

What did you do in the morning?

What did you do at lunchtime?

What did you do in the afternoon?

Who did you play with?

What was the weather like?

What was the best thing that happened?

What was the worst thing that happened?

What were you looking forward to?

Copymaster 73

Memory time line 7–11 years

7 years old	8 years old	9 years old

10 years old	11 years old

Memory jogger

A pet	A new baby
A row	Disaster

Moving home or school	An accident
A strange person	A lie

Gnome's diary

Wednesday 19 June

Thursday 20 June

Monday 17 June

Today we found a huge spear. It will be very useful for defending ourselves. The humans call it a knitting needle. In the afternoon we slept under a warm car. It was very cosy but smelled badly. We raided the dustbins and the foxes got the blame. Drank cream from the milk bottles left on the doorsteps.

Tuesday 18 June

REDRAFTING AND PROOFREADING

This final section is concerned with developing the process of writing and looks at the importance of redrafting as a way of improving what has been written. Copymasters focus upon making texts more interesting through the careful selection of words and structure. The children are invited to improve first drafts of stories and poetry, and to write from a brainstorming session. The skills of proofreading are also highlighted through exercises that require punctuation and spelling to be checked.

Copymaster 83 directs children into the early stages of using a response partner to assist in redrafting and proofreading. There is also help with making a simple book and a chance for children to invite their families to help them with writing. There are two self-assessment copymasters for children to choose from; for the teacher **Copymaster 97** (Writing record) could be used for every child and maintained as part of official school records. It is suggested that this is used each term to assist in recording what the child can do and to focus the teacher's mind on what is needed next to assist development. **Copymaster 98** (Writing record prompt sheet) has key words on it that may be useful when completing the writing record. The words on the prompt sheet should be updated in terms of National Curriculum requirements as and when changes are made to Level Descriptions/Statements of Attainment and National Assessments.

Copymaster 77 (Boring sentences 1)
The children read the sentences and then make changes to improve them and make them more interesting. The children could do any of the following:

- **Change** a word – so 'The tramp came down the road' becomes 'The tramp hobbled down the road'
- **Add in** words – so 'The tramp hobbled down the road' becomes 'The old tramp hobbled down the dusty road'
- **Add on** words – so 'The tramp came down the road' becomes 'The tramp came down the road shouting for joy'.

The children should compare their sentences to see who has made the best improvements. The first one has been done for them.

Copymaster 78 (Capitals, full stops and 'and')
This is the start of Simon's story. He has used too many 'and's. Let the children change his writing to get rid of some of these 'and's and add in full stops and capital letters. This could be done individually, after which children could compare and discuss so that agreement can be reached on what should be changed.

Copymaster 79 (Fill the gaps)
To practise selecting words carefully the children, in pairs, read the passage and then insert what they feel may be the most effective word. Pairs should compare and discuss their choices. Some of the spaces might be filled by one word, some by two or three.

Copymaster 80 (Poem draft 1)
This copymaster shows the first draft of a poem. The children have to read it through and then make any changes they wish to, in order to help improve it. Changes should then be discussed and justified. The children should focus on changing words to improve them.

Copymaster 81 (Story draft 1)
This copymaster is a first draft of the opening to a story. On this draft children should make changes to improve the story. In particular they should look out for repetition and add in words for description.

Copymaster 82 (Speech bubbles)
Children should look carefully at the pictures on this copymaster and then add in what they think the people are saying. This activity should be built on at Key Stage 2 by children circling the actual words that their characters speak when they write. Individuals or groups should be shown how to set out speech marks once they can identify which words a character says.

Copymaster 83 (Response partner)
A response partner is used to test out a piece of writing. The idea is that once the children have written a first draft they read their work to a friend who will be their response partner. The response partner has to let the child know what works well in their piece of writing as well as helping them make any improvements. The directions on the copymaster should prove useful in establishing response partners in the classroom. Once the children have used their response partners to help with the revising they can then work together on the proofreading. Point out to the children that they should check their writing with the teacher before publishing!

This activity helps children to develop the ability to revise their own work and to critically comment on the strengths and weaknesses of writing. The children may wish to fill in suggestions at the bottom of the page following a discussion on what helps most when working together. The filled-in copymaster should then be kept as a reminder of the procedure.

Copymaster 84 (Make a book)
This copymaster gives simple instructions for making a booklet and could be used in school or taken home for parents to help in the activity.

Copymaster 85 (Family story)
This copymaster is an invitation for people at home, whether families or friends, to write a story with the children. The children could begin the story, with those at home then joining in and adding more writing as well as illustrations. These stories could be discussed in school and would make an interesting book or scrapbook collection – especially for parents to see on parents' evenings.

Copymaster 86 (My writing)
This is a self-assessment sheet for younger children to complete by colouring in the appropriate face and adding their name, the date and their comments on their own favourite piece of writing.

Copymaster 87 (Brainstorm)
This copymaster shows a handwritten brainstorming session for stimulating a piece of writing on owls. The children need to think carefully about the intended audience (this could be written for another class or to take home) and the main pieces of information that are mentioned before they use the brainstorm as a basis for their own writing. Children should decide whether they need to include all the information shown on the brainstorm and whether to include illustrations as well as writing.

The second half of the copymaster contains a blank brainstorming model for the children to use when gathering information on a writing topic of the teacher's or their own choice.

Copymaster 88 (Boring sentences 2)
The children should read and then improve these sentences by making **changes** to dull words, **adding in** words to improve description and **adding on** words to extend the description. They should beware of adding too much, which could detract from the quality of the writing.

Copymaster 89 (Boring words)
This is a copy of Joanna's opening to a story. The children should focus upon improving the **choice** of words by redrafting, making changes on the copymaster first.

Copymaster 90 (Proofread)
The children should proofread this story opening, checking carefully for spelling mistakes and adding capital letters, full stops, speech marks and paragraphs. They could then complete the story.

Copymaster 91 (Computer error 2)
This copymaster should be used like a cloze procedure. My computer has lost some of the words and phrases from this story. The children should discuss and decide what are the best words to use to fill in the gaps – sometimes two or three words are needed. Children could then complete the story.

Copymasters 92 and 93 (Poem drafts 2 and 3)
These copymasters show the first drafts of two new poems. The children should work over the drafts in pairs, improving the quality by writing in the spaces between the lines, crossing out words and underlining or circling parts they wish to improve.

Copymasters 94 and 95 (Story drafts 2 and 3)
These copymasters show the first drafts of parts of a story. The children should work over the drafts, polishing the prose by making changes on the copymasters. These changes should then be discussed as a class. **Copymaster 95** also needs proofreading for spelling mistakes and punctuation.

Copymaster 96 (Self-assessment)
This copymaster could be used at the end of each term for older children to summarise how they consider they have developed as writers and how they would like to develop in the future. The copymaster could be used as part of the termly 'writing conference' (see pages ix–x). The teacher will need to discuss with the children during a class session the sorts of things they might write on their sheets. It may be useful to attach the copymaster to an example of the child's work.

Copymaster 97 (Writing record)
This copymaster may be used by the teacher to make notes on the child's on-going development, informed by termly discussions with the child (see the notes on the writing conference on pages ix–x) and general classroom observations. **Copymaster 98** acts as a prompt sheet to help the teacher complete this record.

The writing record can be used for children who have just begun to write as well as experienced writers. The teacher will need to listen carefully to children talking to gain a sense of their ability to compose and to fill in the 'content' section. In the 'conventions' section the teacher may wish to distinguish between the various spelling stages – scribbling, letter shapes, using properly formed letters, sound/symbol correspondence, spelling using phonics, spelling from visual memory. The teacher may wish to note whether children play at and enjoy writing. Do children know the difference between drawing and writing? Can they read back their own writing?

Copymaster 98 (Writing record prompt sheet)
This copymaster highlights key considerations and aspects to look for when completing the termly writing record on **Copymaster 97**. Teachers may wish to add in key words or phrases from the Level Descriptions/ Statements of Attainment to assist in the on-going monitoring of children's development in terms of the National Curriculum. They may also wish to add any key aspects that National Assessments are highlighting.

FURTHER IDEAS

Write in front of the children on an easel, flipchart, board or OHP. As you reread what has been written encourage the children to suggest improvements.

Draw children's attention to well-used words and phrases they come across in their reading.

Create worksheets of poorly written pieces of writing that need improving.

Encourage children to reread and make improvements to their own writing.

Read out aloud examples of children's work and ask for suggestions to improve weaker parts.

Encourage the children to work in story circles. In the circle the children take it in turn to read aloud their stories while their friends make suggestions for improvement.

Create worksheets that focus on different proofreading aspects – speech marks, paragraphs, capital letters, etc. Use these to highlight features that certain children need to address in their own writing. Encourage children to check their writing for a limited number of such features.

Boring sentences 1

1   The dog came down the street.

The brown dog ran yapping down the high street.

2   The girl picked up the ball.

3   He said that he had seen a horse.

4   The apples were nice.

5   The snow fell on the trees.

6   The cat sat on me.

7   The bus went through the tunnel.

8   In the cave it was dark.

Copymaster 77

Full stops and 'and'

The cruel crow

early one morning sam went out and saw a crow and the crow was sitting in a tree and waiting and simon went back to the house for his breakfast and the crow saw him go into the house and thought now I can fly down and pinch some beans from the garden and he flew down and pecked the beans and peapods and just at that moment simon came out of the house and he saw the crow and he tried to shoo it away and the crow did not like this and it pecked simon on the nose and simon got really angry

Copymaster 78

Fill the gaps

Sally had _____ wanted a puppy. When it was her _____ birthday her Dad took her to the _____ shop. He bought her a _____ puppy.

Sally called the _____ Noodles. It had a _____ nose and a _____ tail.

That afternoon she took Noodles for a _____ in the park. She had _____ ball to throw for Noodles. But he wouldn't _____ back. He had run away. Sally searched _____ for Noodles.

When she got home Sally had been _____. But as she came up the path to her house who should come _____ out to meet her? Yes, it was naughty Noodles.

Copymaster 79

97

Poem draft 1

The big snow flakes fall

on the ground

they look like big lumps

as they drop down.

Snow covers the cars

in a cover of snow.

It is like white powder

on the lawn.

The puddles are frozen

and look like icy plates.

The snow crunches

beneath my feet.

The cat leaves small paw prints

and she comes home.

Copymaster 80

 **Story draft 1**

Once upon a time there was a woman who was lonely. She lived all by herself in the middle of a wood. She was quite lonely. She had no one to talk to from morning till night. She lived all by herself in a cottage in the middle of a wood.

Late one night she was in her sitting room. She had just lit a candle. The flame was moving and the shadows were moving. She moved across the room and she picked up her embroidery. She was making a pretty lace handkerchief. It was pretty.

She sat in front of the fire and watched the shadows move. The flames were moving. She picked up her pretty embroidery and began to sew. As she sewed she heard a big noise. It came from the roof. It sounded like someone with big feet was moving on the big roof. She wondered what on earth was going on.

Copymaster 81

99

Speech bubbles

Response partner

How to be a good response partner

1 Together, read your friend's writing carefully.

2 Now point out all the words, ideas and parts that you think are good.

3 Ask questions about the writing.

4 Point out any places where you think the writing could be made better.

5 Discuss ideas for changes and let the writer make the final decision.

Once the work has been redrafted, it needs to be proofread.

1 Put a circle around any spelling mistakes. Check these in a word book, dictionary or ask a friend.

2 Underline any places where you think the punctuation (full stops, capitals, question marks, speech marks) is wrong. Correct it.

3 Discuss the layout to make the work easy to read and attractive to look at.

Now your writing is ready to **publish**.

Make a book

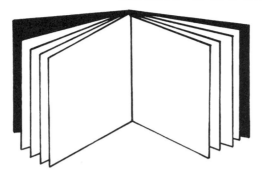

1 Take some sheets of paper and put a cover on the outside. Fold them carefully.

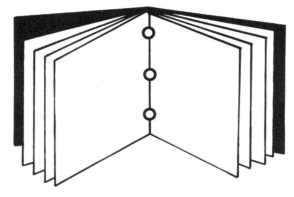

2 Make three holes.

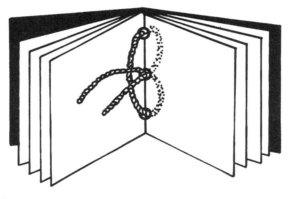

3 Sew the pages together.

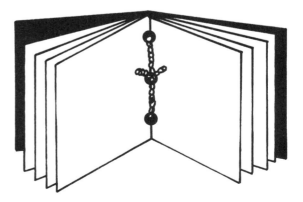

4 Tie a knot in the thread.

Copymaster 84

102

Family story

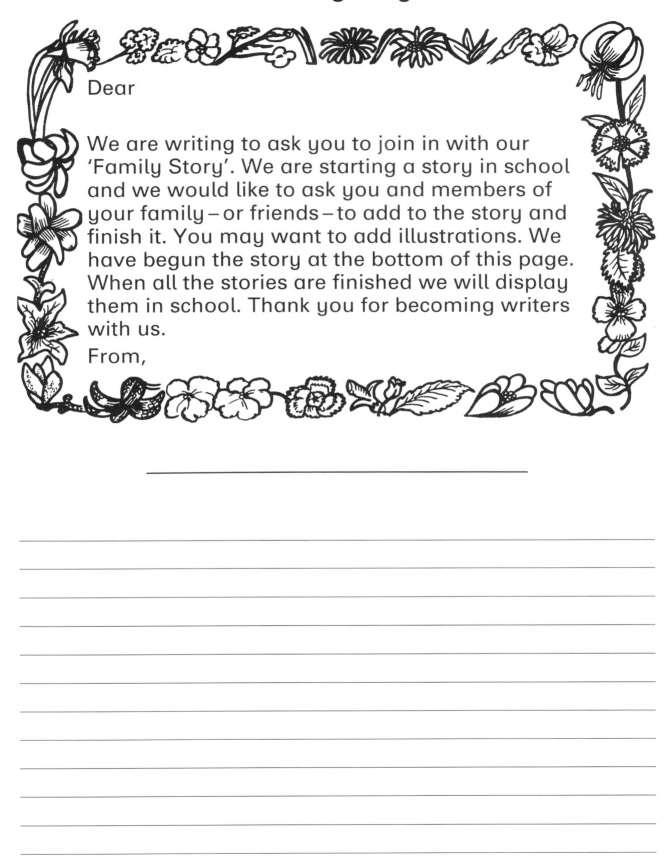

Dear

We are writing to ask you to join in with our 'Family Story'. We are starting a story in school and we would like to ask you and members of your family – or friends – to add to the story and finish it. You may want to add illustrations. We have begun the story at the bottom of this page. When all the stories are finished we will display them in school. Thank you for becoming writers with us.

From,

_____

_____
_____
_____
_____
_____
_____
_____
_____
_____
_____

Copymaster 85

My writing

Name –
Date –

I enjoy writing – stories

news

information

letters

poems

about myself

about school

I can – write neatly

join up

spell most words

use a dictionary

use a word book

use full stops

use capital letters

use question marks

I can – redraft

proofread

My best piece of writing is about –

I like it because –

Brainstorm

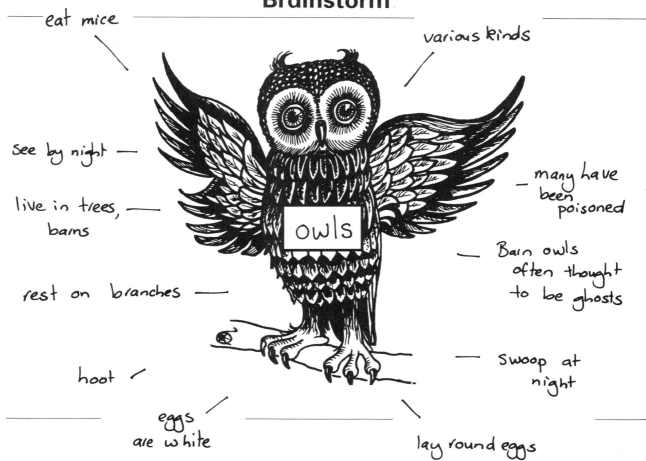

eat mice

various kinds

see by night

live in trees, barns

many have been poisoned

rest on branches

Barn owls often thought to be ghosts

hoot

swoop at night

eggs are white

lay round eggs

owls

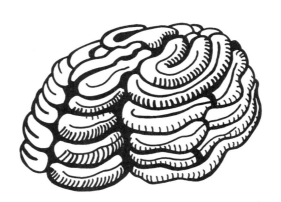

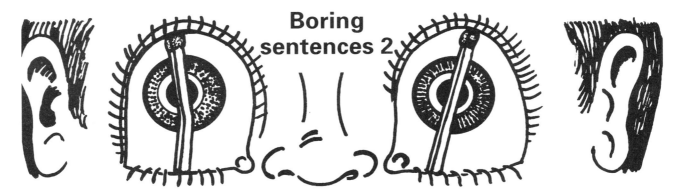

Boring sentences 2

1   The farmer looked at the bull as it came towards him.

2   The spacecraft door opened and out came a creature.

3   The waves banged on the rocks.

4   A car came round the corner.

5   George ran after the man.

6   The dog showed its teeth and growled.

7   The moon shone down on the thieves.

8   The boat came up the beach and the smugglers dropped out.

9   In my dream I saw a shape.

10 The teacher spoke to the noisy class.

Copymaster 88

Boring words

There was no noise in the classroom. On the wall was a drawing of a big monster with a big mouth full of big teeth. Suddenly it winked its horrid eye at me. It came alive and got off the wall. It came across the room and went through the window. Joel and I went after it.

We found it by the swings. It said in a funny voice, 'Leave me alone'. Now we were closer we could see it had funny bits of hair on it. Its eyes looked odd too. It was quite small with nice feet like a bird's. It smiled at us. Its teeth were not straight. 'I am fed up,' it said in a low voice. It started to cry.

Proofread

early one morning mr fox woke up and he picked

up his bag and went out to look for something to

eat he had not gone far when he herd a

bumblebee buzzing so he grabbed it and shoved it

into his bag he walked on till he came to a little

cotage and he knoked at the door and went

straight in may i leave my bag here while i visit

mr couson cuthbert asked the fox of course you

can answerred the little old lady very well siad the

fox but mind you dont look in my bag so off went

the fox down the lane now no sooner had he

disapeered out of sihght than she began to grow

curioius she though ill take one liitle look it wont

matter so she peeped into the bag and thre

bumblebee came flying out it went straight into

her farm yard where her cockral ate it up in one

gulp.

Computer error 2

Sally   hands into her pockets and set off down the street. The wind blew and a

dampened her coat. What a terrible holiday it was turning out to be. Mum had promised her

beaches but all they had had was rain and pebbly beaches covered in and crisp packets.

Sally stopped at the amusement arcade and in. She hadn't got much money left but at least inside. She pushed her way th double doors and into the warmth, the lights and sound of the machines. At first she round and watched other children playing on the machines. She watched and waited by a one-armed bandit machine which took 50p pieces. 50p was all she had left.

A boy with   hair had been playing on the machine and when he left it Sally moved forwards to

. She pushed the coin into the slot and

she pulled the lever. The cogs spun, the lights   and the machine

To win she needed three of the same fruit to come up. First an apple appeared. Then a second. Finally, a third. She'd won! The machine made a strange   noise and began to pump money out. She had won. £10!

She left the arcade with her pockets and her   with the excitement. She couldn't tell her mum. She disapproved of gambling. What on earth was she to do?

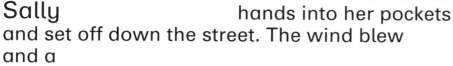

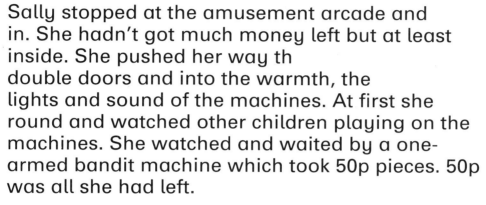

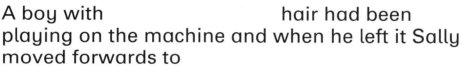

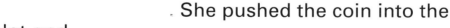

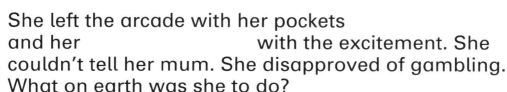

Copymaster 91

Poem draft 2

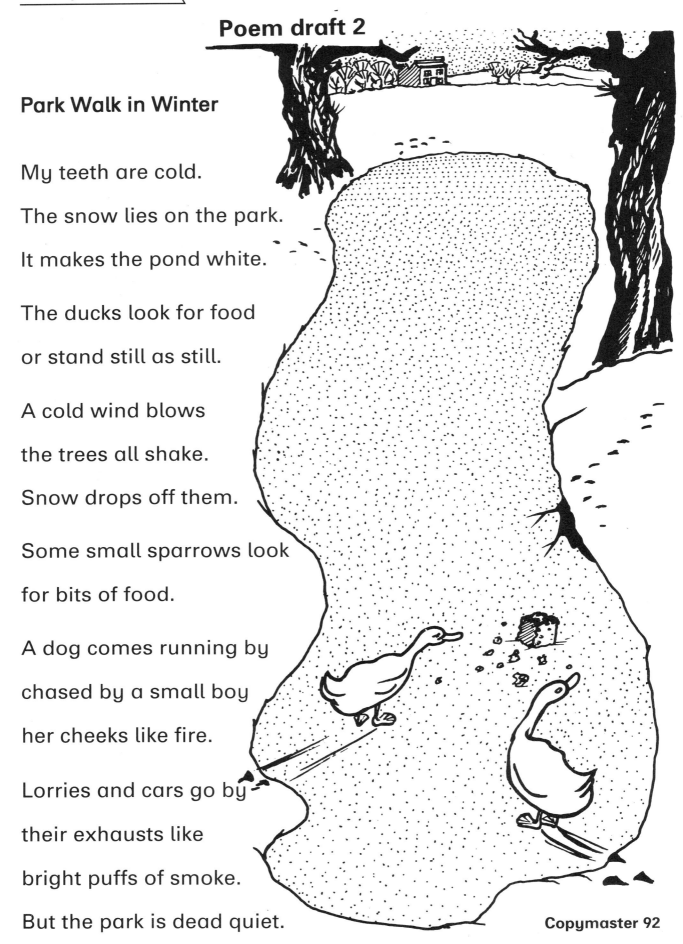

Park Walk in Winter

My teeth are cold.

The snow lies on the park.

It makes the pond white.

The ducks look for food

or stand still as still.

A cold wind blows

the trees all shake.

Snow drops off them.

Some small sparrows look

for bits of food.

A dog comes running by

chased by a small boy

her cheeks like fire.

Lorries and cars go by

their exhausts like

bright puffs of smoke.

But the park is dead quiet.

Copymaster 92

110

Poem draft 3

Follow me

Follow me to a place

where the trees have loads of fruit.

Follow me to a land

where there are lots of big trees

that all can move and talk to you.

Follow me to a country

where even the hedges are smiling at everybody.

Follow me to a world

that is made of all the funny things

that have been going on around here.

Follow me to a room

where the curtains hold each other's hands.

Follow me to a house

where the pots and pans are running

about everywhere saying things.

Copymaster 93

111

Story draft 2

The streets were empty but Sally thought that she was being followed. She thought that she could hear the noises of someone who was following her all the time. She turned around now and then but she could not see anyone. At the corner of South Street she went round quickly and hid behind a big dustbin. She could hear her heart beating as she was crouching down. She was trying to hold her breath. Then she heard the sound of someone's footsteps coming down the road quietly. Whoever it was paused by the big dustbin. Sally could see a pair of black shoes. They were smelly. She felt really scared in case she was spotted. Suddenly a hand shot down and grabbed her by the collar. She was pulled to her feet and a horrid face pressed close to hers. 'Now, tell me where it is,' asked the person. But Sally hadn't got the faintest clue what she was talking about.

Copymaster 94

Story draft 3

Tom ran down to the classroom but he was very late. Mrs

Snell had already begun the lessin. He tried to creep in

without being seen but she roared at him what on earth are

you doing arriving so late Im soory he replide but the bus

was late. She made a noise of disgust and so he sat down

in his seat, sitting next to him was a girl that he had never

seen before she had long black hair tied into a pigtale.

Toms fingers wanted to pull it like a church bell pull. Mrs

snell was telling them what to do and the girl next to tom

was already writing loads. he looked over at what she was

doing and saw that it was a story. it could of been really

good but tom knudged her and ink spilt across the table

and all across her work it also dropped onto her new school

clothes. She turned to tom with her eyes burning with

crossness You idiot she shouted. The next thing they new

Mrs Snell had walked over to them

Copymaster 95

Self-assessment

| GOOD ← | OK | BAD |

List the types of writing that you prefer

Punctuation checklist
Paragraphs ☐
Speech marks ☐
Commas ☐
Exclamation marks ☐
Question marks ☐
Capital letters ☐
Full stops ☐
Apostrophes ☐

Name your best piece and say why you like it

Can you change your writing depending on who you are writing for? ☐

Do you plan before writing? ☐

How do you help as a response partner?

Can you redraft your own work? ☐

Can you proofread? ☐

Is your best writing neat? ☐

What sort of writing do you have the best ideas for?

Do you use the wordprocessor for writing? ☐

What is the next aspect you would like to improve?

How can your teacher help?

Any other comments about yourself as a writer?

Copymaster 96

Writing record

Name   Date

Title of writing

Context

Child's response

Content

Conventions

Process

Suggested level

Next development

Writing record prompt sheet

Context
Was this aided or unaided? Was this a first draft?

Child's response
Does the child enjoy writing/discussing writing?

Content
Good ideas, logical and chronological flow, appropriate style, good use of story grammar (well-described setting, engaging opening, believable characters, interesting events, a main dilemma, defined ending), engages interest, appropriate for purpose and audience? Is writing lively, honest, vigorous? Does the child play with language to create verbal effects? Does the child use imagery? Are the stories and poems moving? Is information writing clear and interesting? Is writing confident? Is writing structured effectively? Is the child's use of vocabulary appropriate, broad and interesting? Does the child write honestly and directly, convey meaning clearly and effectively, produce sustained and well-organised writing.

Conventions
Spelling stage, handwriting, punctuation (full stops, capitals, question marks, exclamation marks, commas, speech marks). Command of Standard English? Can the child set out a letter? Use of appropriate layout/paragraphs? Has the child moved beyond using 'and' repeatedly? Use of sentences in which subject/verb agree? Use of parts of speech correctly and effectively?

Process
Can the child redraft? Can the child spot areas that are effective and identify areas that could be improved, make improvements independently, discuss writing and justify redraftings, identify spelling, punctuation and grammar mistakes? Does the child proofread and make effective changes? Does the child plan and use a range of strategies for starting writing? Is the child a good response partner? Does the child use appropriate terms to discuss their writing?

Suggested level
Using the evidence of the child's writing during this term suggest the relevant NC level. Use the notes from any national assessment as guidance for the key determining factors.

Next development
Discuss and identify several areas for development with the child. Review these at the next conference session.

Copymaster 98

SPEECH AND DRAMA

ANN JONES
AND
ROBERT CHEESEMAN

EDITED BY

JOHN NICHOLAS AND KEN PICKERING

Dramatic Lines*

DRAMATIC LINES, TWICKENHAM, ENGLAND
Speech and Drama
text copyright © Ann Jones and Robert Cheeseman 2004

Dramatic Lines
PO Box 201
Twickenham
TW2 5RQ
England

A CIP record for this book is
available from the British Library

ISBN 1 904557 15 5

Speech and Drama
first published in 2004
by
Dramatic Lines
Twickenham England

Printed by The Dramatic Lines Press
Twickenham England

FOREWORD

This **SPEECH AND DRAMA Handbook** is one of a series primarily designed to support students and teachers preparing for examinations from the Drama and Speech syllabus of Trinity College, *London.*

However, the Dramatic Lines Handbooks have much wider applications. Not only do they provide accessible and practical advice to students working towards ANY examination in Drama, Speech, Communication or Performing Arts, they also give invaluable help to those who wish to use their skills in a professional capacity as performers, teachers or communicators.

The Handbooks are quite literally something to keep to hand whenever you are working towards an important examination, performance, audition or presentation and you will find that they become your constant companions for a life in the Performance and Communications Arts.

Ken Pickering

Ken Pickering

Chief Examiner for Drama and Speech at
Trinity College, *London* and Professor of Arts Education
at the Institute for Arts in Therapy and Education

CONTENTS

INTRODUCTION

This handbook is designed to provide practical advice to teachers and students working in the fields of speech and drama.

It will be especially helpful to those preparing work for examinations since almost all of the chapters directly address examination requirements, giving detailed consideration to what candidates should think about when preparing for each area under discussion.

However, the book will also have a far wider application, offering ideas and information that will stimulate and develop student abilities within every branch of speech and drama.

Ann Jones and Robert Cheeseman

1   WHAT IS 'SPEECH AND DRAMA'?

'Be still when you have nothing to say; when genuine passion moves you, say what you've got to say, and say it hot.'

D H Lawrence

'Speech and Drama' is a term that has been around for a long time, and over the years it has come to mean different things to different people.

During the latter part of the 20th century the term gradually became unfashionable in certain quarters: for a significant number it carried negative overtones, associated with what had come to be regarded as an outmoded approach, putting emphasis on style rather than substance. Some people even accused it of encouraging class divisiveness. Because of this many deliberately shunned the term, choosing instead labels such as 'performing arts', 'communication skills' and 'theatre studies'.

Now that we have moved into the 21st century, it seems that most people are prepared to drop such prejudices, and there is a widespread acknowledgement that the label 'Speech and Drama' is a usefully descriptive one that can be employed without reserve, free of irrelevant negative implications.

> The word **speech** comes from an old English word *spec the utterance of words or sentences* and most usually refers to our *ability to express thoughts or feelings by articulate sounds*

> The word **drama** is derived from the Greek word *dran to do.* The word originally referred to *a deed or the process of doing.*

Basically then, 'Speech and Drama' is a classification that embraces two immeasurably common activities: **talking** and **behaving** – activities that all of us are involved in, almost all of our waking lives. We are constantly **saying** things and **doing** things. Therefore, the subject 'Speech and Drama' is concerned with the most central occupations of our lives, and that explains why **speech** and **drama** are among the oldest disciplines of study in civilization.

Q Why make a study of two such natural processes, engaged in by all of us, so spontaneously and regularly?

Look again at the definitions above. The immense importance of our talking and behaviour lies in the fact that we convey thoughts and feelings through those activities. Whether we like it or not, a huge amount of our behaviour

2

and speaking, gives off signals that are perceived by others to carry meaning. We are all constantly communicating, sometimes deliberately – sometimes not, sometimes effectively – sometimes not.

Most of us would like to try to ensure that we communicate as well as possible, and this desire has stimulated a systematic study and practice of speech and drama from earliest times.

Throughout history the arts of speaking and acting have been judged to be of immense value, since they are the most basic means through which we communicate with each other: no tools or instruments are needed other than your own body, and the air and space that you inhabit.

ORATORY

Oratory was in widespread practice long before the ancient rhetoricians developed a theory and a vocabulary for rhetoric. In fact ancient rhetoricians developed their theories and definitions through their observation that some orators were effective and others were not and gradually a set of principles for successful communication was developed.

To the ancient Greeks oratory was among the noblest of arts, and oration was the aristocrat of all forms of public speaking. The orator, among the Greeks and Romans 2000 years ago and more, was highly respected and greatly admired, a citizen of unusual ability and influence.

Aristotle defined oratory as:

> *'the faculty of finding all the means of persuasion'*

Cicero viewed it as:

> *'the art of persuasion'*

Quintilian considered it to be:

> *'the art of speaking well'*

Delivery, as one of the five canons of rhetoric, primarily concerned itself with effectiveness of speaking, and the variations in voice and body movements such speaking required. In essence, it dealt with the speaker's ability to manipulate auditory and visual processes to enable him/her to effectively convey his/her thoughts, argument and feelings to an audience.

The actual term 'speech and drama' has been recognized as a combination title for many years.

Here are 4 examples of its earliest uses:

1 **Elsie Fogerty**, the famous British teacher of voice and dramatic diction was a major figure in theatrical training. She taught elocution at the Crystal Palace School of Art and Literature in 1889 before joining Sir Frank Benson's London School of Acting. Then in 1906 she founded the Central School of Speech Training and Dramatic Art in London, which was later to become known as The Central School of Speech and Drama. Among her pupils were Sybil Thorndike, Peggy Ashcroft, John Gielgud, and Laurence Olivier. She wrote several treatises, the best known is *The Speaking of English Verse* (1923).

2 **Rudolf Steiner**, the Austrian-born scientist and founder of anthroposophy (a movement founded to meet our '*hunger for the spirit and freedom from the fetters of a soul destroying materialism*') gave a series of lectures in 1924 entitled *Speech and Drama*. These were subsequently published in 1959 as a book of the same title.

The book is filled with insights leading to a deeper understanding of the act of speaking and the art of acting. *Speech and Drama* is still available (see FURTHER READING).

Steiner also wrote a book on the art of speaking, suggesting that speech can be brought to life by an exploration of how the audible sound of speech is the end result of an inner process. This book contrasted markedly with the widespread belief that good speaking was entirely a matter of correct placement in the mouth.

3   **Rose Bruford** was a student at Central School of Speech and Drama in 1921 and wrote a book *Speech and Drama* for teachers in 1948.   Two years later she founded the Rose Bruford College of Speech and Drama.

4   *The Society of Teachers of Speech and Drama* was established soon after the Second World War (through an amalgamation of two much earlier Associations) to protect the professional interests of qualified, specialist teachers of speech and drama, to encourage good standards of teaching and to promote the study and knowledge of speech and dramatic art in all its various forms.

Details of the Society can be found on its website: **http://www.stsd.org.uk**

2   EXAMINATIONS IN SPEECH AND DRAMA

'The unexamined life is not worth living.'

Socrates

A rigorous **examination syllabus** in Speech and Drama such as the one provided by Trinity College, *London* offers a systematic scheme for development of personal communication skills. In addition, examiners' personalized written assessments provide learners and teachers with profitable, impartial, professional feedback.

Think for a moment: when you attempt to communicate, you use a variety of visual and audible signals that you hope will have a productive impact on one or more receivers.

Q How can you know how successful you're being?

You can only guess – unless you are given an objective specialist response. By furnishing students and teachers with an appraisal of their endeavours, examiners provide an invaluable service. The most useful assessments are, without doubt, those that identify effective aspects of performance as well as elements that could be improved in one or more ways. Trinity is committed to a belief that success can only be built upon success, and that is why Trinity examiners invariably, and particularly at foundation stages, try to encourage candidates through identifying their strengths and potential strengths.

Most importantly, **a progressive examination programme** provides a unique pathway through which students are able to develop their communication abilities. As examination levels progress, so assignments and targets become gradually more demanding, encouraging students, in a gently stepped manner, to extend their competences.

The Trinity syllabus provides a comprehensive programme of nine Graded steps followed by Professional Certificates and Diplomas – catering for everyone, from the very beginner to those of the highest levels of capability.

Because speaking is such an everyday activity, it is easy to forget that for all of us it was once a learned activity; and any learned activity can, through systematic practice, be developed and improved through acquisition of further skills and greater levels of skill. All of us, however experienced, can learn to express ourselves more effectively. The ancient Greeks realized how vital effective communication was to their society.

Q   Can it be of any less importance to our own?

3   POETRY SPEAKING

'Poetry is what gets lost in translation.'

Robert Frost

When aiming to improve spoken communication skills, poetry speaking is an extremely useful starting point.

Q   What do we mean by 'poetry'?

It is generally agreed that it is impossible to precisely define **poetry** although it certainly refers to language that is carefully designed to have an impact upon its receiver/s through its meaning/s, its sounds, and the ways in which those sounds relate to each other through phenomena such as rhyme, metre and rhythm. The vast majority of poems need to be spoken before they can be truly appreciated. They require, as the great Welsh poet **Dylan Thomas** put it, *'the colour of saying'*.

The **speaking of poetry** (**heightened language**) will therefore always encourage a more colourful utterance. If you study the very influential books of the famous voice teacher **Cicely Berry** such as *Your Voice and How to Use It* and *Voice and the Actor* (see FURTHER READING), you will see that the essence of her work is the use of poetry to extend the range and scope of speaking capacity.

If we confine our speaking to everyday utilitarian phrases such as, '*I think I'll have another cup of coffee*' or '*Did you see that programme on television last night?*' there will be no incentive to develop our speaking parameters.

Whereas, to do any justice at all to phrases such as:

> *To see a World in a Grain of Sand*
> *And a Heaven in a Wild Flower,*
> *Hold Infinity in the palm of your hand*
> *And Eternity in an hour,*
>
> William Blake

. . . . . you will have to find much more expressiveness than is required for mere phrases of chat.

Chat is important – it is part of spoken communication but it is not sufficient if we want to express anything beyond the utilitarian.

When the playwright **Christopher Fry** was asked why he wrote his plays in poetry, he replied that poetry was '*truer to the way our minds work*'. All of us think in a kind of poetry, our minds dancing in images, memories, fantasies . . . . . in fact, our unspoken thoughts hardly ever resemble ordered, structured prose.

Dylan Thomas, when speaking of his childhood, once declared:

> *'The first poems I knew were nursery rhymes . . . .*
> *I had come to love just the words of them, the*
> *words alone. And these words were, to me, as the*
> *notes of bells, the sounds of musical instruments,*
> *the noises of wind, sea and rain . . . . . 'Ride a*
> *cockhorse to Banbury Cross' was haunting to me*
> *who did not know then what a cockhorse was or*
> *cared a damn where Banbury Cross might be.'*

When children first learn poetry

Young people should always enjoy their poetry, and communicate their pleasure with face and voice.

When they first learn poetry, children often enjoy moving and employ supportive gestures to assist their memory.

Encourage good stance and posture – but if hands want to react to the words and this creates enjoyment, don't suppress it. Better to have an expressive child than a stiff restricted delivery.

➡️ TRY THIS: When children start to prepare for examinations, you might ask them to consider a television performance. Only the head and shoulders are visible and the poem must be spoken to the camera – any excessive movement or action means the camera has to move back and cannot focus fully on the face (contemporary children usually appreciate this analogy).

Short lively poems should be used at first – ones that do not take a great deal of learning.

Look at the work of **Rodney Bennett, Elizabeth Fleming, Edward Lear, Spike Milligan, Judith Nicholls, Michael Rosen, Clive Sansom** and **Shel Silverstein**.

In addition, you can write your own jingles for individual sounds.

Here is an example for the letter A:

Ann went to Africa and met Andrew Ant,
Andrew had a top hat on, and some Amber pants.
"You look very smart today", Ann to Andrew said.
Andrew raised his top hat, and oh! His hair was RED!

Ann Jones

➩ THINK ABOUT: **Key words**. Help the children to recognize the important word in a line and encourage them to stress it if necessary. Remind them that small words, such as <u>and</u>, <u>but</u> and <u>a</u>, do NOT require pressure. Children are often over-aware of metrical stress and sometimes use it too much, which tends to distort the meaning and cause the poem to lack fluency. Thinking about the stress of key words, should enable them to avoid metrical pressure. If singsong delivery is an additional problem, thinking about the key words should also help them to overcome this tendency.

➩ THINK ABOUT: **The meaning of the poem,** and ensure that words are understood and can be explained.

➩ THINK ABOUT: **Pitch changes and the use of pause**. Work on the 'happy and sad' principle, choosing poems that have changing moods so that voices can be raised and lowered. Pause should be used to allow the audience time to enjoy the poem (see III *PAUSING* p.118). Remember also the pause between the title and the first line - initially children can count to two after the title.

NOTE: This training in modulation will be of great benefit as they mature.

➩ THINK ABOUT: **Stance and posture**. Good habits are better learnt at a young age. If body control is encouraged early, it will prepare students for when they move into audience-based drama.

➡ THINK ABOUT: **Eye contact**. If the poem is humorous or it needs to be shared with the audience, where should the speaker look? If the performance is on a stage or platform, consider that the head should move no more than 40 degrees either side, otherwise the vocal projection is weakened and scattered. If a poem is about a memory or involves the imagination, the atmosphere would usually be hindered by personal eye contact – better to look forward to where the voice is to be projected. If this causes actual eye involvement with the audience, then encourage students to raise their eyes slightly in order to avoid this. Beware of lifting the chin though as this can cause vocal strain.

➡ THINK ABOUT: **Suitable poems**. These are continually being produced and can be found in bookshops, libraries and via the Internet.

Useful publications include: *1000 Poems* (Evans); *A Very First Poetry Book* and *A First Poetry Book*, etc. (Oxford University Press); *Read Me 1 and Read Me 2*; *A Poem for Every Day of the Year* (Macmillan Children's Books); collections by **Barbara Ireson**; *Skool Verse* and *More Skool Verse* by **Jennifer Curry**; *Around the World in Eighty Poems* by **J** and **G Curry** (Beaver and Puffin Books).

Teachers and pupils should constantly be on the look out for enjoyable verse. Choose simple themes which require imagination, or to which children can relate.

Later, when vocal control and imagination are developing, a move can be made to poetry with more thought and depth. Look at the work of **Charles Causley, John Walsh,** and anthologies by **Anne Harvey**.

More mature students will often enjoy searching for poetry that they can understand and appreciate but the teacher can guide them by suggesting modern poets such as: **Charles Causley, John Walsh, Vernon Scannell, Elizabeth Jennings** and anthologies by **Anthony Thwaite**.

Sometimes students can be encouraged to create a thematic anthology using TITLES – such as: *Love, The Countryside, Animals, War and Peace, 1st World War, Unusual Characters, Poets of my Country* or PERIODS – such as: *Romantic.*

➭ THINK ABOUT: **Using mime and improvisation** – especially if imagination is poor. The poem can be used as a base for a situation or mood, the student acting out the poem's ideas without using the actual words. Suitable poems include: *Bedtime, Boredom* and *Going to Bed* by **Eleanor Farjeon**; *Down by the Pond* and other poems by **A A Milne** (younger children); *The Listeners* and other poems by **Walter De La Mare**; and sports or school

15

poems by **Jennifer Curry** or *Morning Break* and other poems by **Wes Magee**.

NOTE: **Jennifer Curry** and **Wes Magee** both provide a mixture of material suitable for all age levels.

⇨ THINK ABOUT: **When and how to introduce technical matters** – such as the ability to recognise and use particular kinds of verse pause e.g. the **suspensory (suspensive) pause** (see III *PAUSING* p.118 and XVI *USEFUL DEFINITIONS* p.169). As they develop, students can begin to appreciate the difference between **lyrical** and **narrative** poetry (see XVI *USEFUL DEFINITIONS* p.169).

Students who commence poetry speaking when they are older will benefit by work on relaxation, breathing, resonance and articulation, developing basic skills (see the relevant topics in 13 HOW THINGS WORK). They, too, should think about key words and endeavour to maintain the flow of the poem and should be encouraged to think about verbal dynamics and build appropriate atmosphere through word colour.

NOTE: We have already established that speakers can improve their vocal quality, flexibility and range by learning to speak or read poetry aloud.

Whenever we're speaking poetry we should always carefully consider:

- the poet's thoughts and feelings

- the poem's shape and structure

- the pointing of essential thoughts

- pauses peculiar to verse form

- whether or not the speech is clear and reflects the colour found in the imagery and poetic language

- whether or not the voice is produced with good forward tone and full resonance

As students progress they are able to expand their skills and appreciate different types of poetry. Look at the background of each form and be aware of its history and development. All lyrical poetry requires relaxation, poise, good breath control, forward tone, firm articulation and tone colour (see the relevant topics in 13 HOW THINGS WORK).

LYRIC POETRY

Lyric poetry is a name given to a wide range of poetry concerned with a poet's personal thoughts and feelings.

17

These poems usually have a fluency and musicality, employing poetic language and imagery.

> **Always think very carefully about what the poet is feeling and saying** when preparing to speak a pure lyric. If it assists the student's appreciation then look at the poet's life and experiences.

> **Examine the structure**, the length of lines, the metre, rhythmical stress and stanza construction. Note any poetic pauses; metrical, caesural, and suspensory (see III *PAUSING* p.118 and XVI *USEFUL DEFINITIONS* p.169). Any difficult passages should be planned regarding breath control and emphasis should be noted in order to point the meaning. Be sensitive to the musical quality of the poem and use plenty of breath support and resonance, together with an appreciation of alliteration and imagery.

> **Perform with a relaxed stillness** – never intruding between the poet and the meaning. Let the words speak for themselves. Beware of over shaping vowels and lengthening words to excess. Present the poem with sincerity and honesty. Never strive for effect.

> ➤ **Think about eye contact**. If the subject is a personal one or is reflecting a memory, eye contact is not appropriate. Let the eyes and face reflect the thoughts and try to remain in the poet's world.

Care should be taken when choosing a lyric poem because some, although they have lyrical quality, can often include a narrative element, such as **Walter de la Mare's** *The Listeners*. These are sometimes called **lyrical narratives**.

ODE

An ode is usually a poem of some length written in praise of someone or something. It belongs to the lyric category because it is generally of a meditative nature and expressed in an elevated style and formal verse structure. Depending upon its subject matter, an ode should be delivered with a strong sense of personal involvement. Look at famous odes by **John Keats, Percy Bysshe Shelley** and **William Wordsworth**. Notice the construction – length of line, rhyme and rhythm. Appreciate the imagery and be sensitive to the use of alliteration and assonance. Eye contact is NOT used because the poet is concerned with imagination and the communication of thoughts and feelings. You might want to consider other types of odes such as *Sapphic* and *Pindaric* (see *XVI USEFUL DEFINITIONS* p.169). Gesture could be appropriate for the stronger odes, but NEVER employ this if it interferes with the communication of the meaning and the conveying of the poet's feelings.

ELEGY

An elegy is a subjective type of lyric poem that refers to specific people, places or events related to death. This kind of poem should be spoken with an apt sense of grief or sadness and always delivered with genuine sensitivity.

BALLAD

A ballad is a lyric with a musical and dramatic quality, often written with characters and a strong story line. Look at the poet's style and how it is used to create atmosphere. Think carefully about the ballad's structure, its story, the characters and what affect the poem should have on an audience. Find various types of ballads and consider how best to communicate them to an audience. Ballads that are particularly personal rarely require movement. However, a turning of the head or a slight gesture could assist character creation. Endeavour to create an atmosphere, and build up to a climax if necessary.

SONNET

A sonnet is a lyric of fourteen lines and usually has a conventional rhyme scheme (see XVI *USEFUL DEFINITIONS* p.169). When preparing to speak a sonnet a speaker should always ask the question, "What form of sonnet is this?" The form will determine its presentation. An **Italian** sonnet has a natural break after eight lines and this should be observed. A **Shakespearian** has the Italian break plus another one after the twelfth line in order to point the final rhyming couplet. The **Miltonic** has no pause after the eighth line but continues to flow on into the ninth. When these breaks occur, pause for at least 2 - 3 counts. The Italian sestet (final six lines) flows on without reaching a definite climax, whilst the Shakespearian final quatrain builds up to the rhyming couplet that can be spoken with conviction and perhaps extra volume. Some speakers think of the couplet as a kind of punch line! Share the poet's feelings with reflective and natural facial expression, but never be tempted to 'perform'. Think carefully about the sonnet's rhythm. Many of the traditional sonnets are written in **Iambic Pentameter** (see XV *VERSE FORM* p.160) so beware of falling into regular metrical stress. NEVER rush the speaking of a sonnet. If you look for the key word in each line this will aid pace control. Assume that the audience is overhearing the poet's thoughts (you might find it helpful to regard your function as similar to a voice-over). Try sitting, because this often aids relaxation and encourages a natural presentation. Consider placing the seat so that it is facing diagonally, and look slightly sideways towards the audience but not usually with direct eye contact. Involvement with the audience is usually inappropriate – let them overhear! Look at some of the unusual poems of **Gerard Manley Hopkins**, which are often thought of as sonnets, although some have fewer than fourteen lines. Above all you must appreciate a sonnet's condensed form and distilled language. Notice particularly instances of effective alliteration and imagery. Sonnet speaking is usually regarded as the very pinnacle of poetry speaking, requiring the keenest vocal control and complete concentration.

NARRATIVE POETRY

Narrative poetry is simply poetry written primarily to tell a story. Therefore, when it is performed, the communication and characterization of the story should be the speaker's main concern. **Movement and gesture** can often be used to good effect but this should not be at the expense of an appreciation of the style of the verse. The whole poem, or particular sections, can be performed sitting, kneeling or standing. **Eye contact** is essential for the narrative passages – remember you're telling a story! Eye contact should NOT be used when characterizing. A direct and positive approach will assist the communication with the audience. Use a **strong vocal delivery**, endeavouring to create characters through vocal colour and body language – if appropriate. Vary the pace to create suspense, and use plenty of light and shade.

When working on narrative verse, always ask yourself the following 6 key questions:

Q 1   What is the main story line?

Q 2   What **atmosphere** did the poet intend to create?

Q 3   Is the poem humorous or entertaining in a different way?

Q 4   Does the poem have strong dramatic qualities?

Q 5   Does the poem include fear or tension?

Q 6   How does the style of the poem aid the development of the story?

There are various types of narrative poems, and when preparing them for performance, you should always do all you can to appreciate the periods, use of language, form and imagery.

As an example, let us consider a possible approach to Canto 5, lines 87 - 102 of *The Rape of the Lock* by **Alexander Pope**, which is quite a difficult narrative because it is written in rhyming couplets.

The main story line must be firmly communicated whilst the additional embellishments should be taken at a quicker pace. The speaker's eyes can communicate the humour, appealing directly to the audience. Characters need to be played with conviction.

You should focus on an imagined character during the direct speech, and then look at the audience during the following words.

"Now meet thy Fate", incens'd Belinda cry'd,
And drew a deadly Bodkin from her Side.

'The same . . .' commences an embellishment which can be spoken in a more relaxed and chatty manner with good eye contact. Try moving from the main speaking position – for example, explore walking downstage right, then leftwards across the front of the stage.

(The same, his ancient personage to deck,
Her great great grandsire wore about his neck
In three seal-rings which after, melted down,
Form'd a vast buckle for his widow's gown:
Her infant grandame's whistle next it grew,
The bells she jingled, and the whistle blew;
Then in a bodkin grac'd her mother's hairs,
Which long she wore, and now Belinda wears.)

Step back and face as if addressing Belinda. Perhaps use gesture to partly plead - but with false cunning.

"Boast not my fall" (he cry'd)" insulting foe!
Thou by some other shalt be laid as low.
Nor think, to die dejects my lofty mind;
All that I dread, is leaving you behind!

The performer could kneel half way through the penultimate line and remain in that position until the end of this piece of direct speech.

Rather than so, ah let me still survive,
And burn in Cupid's Flames - but burn alive."

Another two powerful examples of narrative poems are **Robert Browning's** *The Pied Piper* and *The Highwayman* by **Alfred Noyes**. Each should have vitality and colour but ensure that this is conveyed by the speaking rather than through excessive movement.

Some modern narratives such as *Private Murder* by **Vernon Scannell** require a variety of pace, pause and power but no movement, although gesture could be used if it aids the speaker.

BLANK VERSE

Blank verse (see XV *VERSE FORM* p.160) is commonly used in narrative poetry, for example look at **John Betjemen's** *Summoned by Bells*. **Iambic pentameter** can sometimes encourage an over-strong metrical stress, so try to convey the flow of the poem and point the meaning. When it is used in verse drama, such as **William Shakespeare's** plays, the basic rhythm should be felt but in no way over-stressed. The character's feelings and meaning provide the key stress words and everything should move towards communicating the underlying emotions of the character. **Caesural pauses** (see XVI *USEFUL DEFINITIONS* p.169) are often useful, and 'sense pauses' provide opportunities for thought change. The verse form should be appreciated but the language should NOT be made to sound 'poetic'! Spoken blank verse should emulate the natural rhythms of English speech, which is why it became the standard metre for poetic drama after its first appearance in 1540.

FREE VERSE

Free verse is easy to recognize because it will have no set length of line, and rhyme will be used either irregularly or not at all. Nonetheless, when studied carefully, the verse will usually offer a spoken rhythm to the speaker – gained through stressing key words and making a natural use of the neutral vowel. Look at the punctuation – sometimes a poet will give clues to the phrasing through this. If there is little or no punctuation, then careful sense phrasing must be employed, and pause used precisely to indicate change of thought. The meaning is all-important but the poetic form should also be conveyed. Use the imagery and phrases to create atmosphere. If the poet suddenly uses a much shorter line, then s/he may wish the speaker to pause after it. If there are several short lines, the poet may wish the pace to increase so that emotion is developed. Speak the poem aloud and explore what the poet is fully saying. Decide why s/he chose to write it in this form rather than in prose. Above all, ensure that you do not let lines run into each other so that prose is created. Feel the flow of each line and how the lines balance. Always look at several works by the same poet so that an understanding of his/her overall approach is achieved. Free verse often shows a marked style and a depth of emotion.

 LOOK AT: The poems of **Ted Hughes, Elizabeth Jennings** and **D H Lawrence**.

NOTE: Verse form is explained in more detail in XV *VERSE FORM* p.160.

To conclude

Each poetic work will have its own special qualities and characteristics. Sometimes the poet will have used an established form such as a traditional sonnet form; and sometimes the poet will have created an original form. Look at the extraordinary and exciting poetry of **E E Cummings**, *Complete Poems* (1968).

It is the speaker's job:

- to investigate all the clues within the writing

- to adopt a state of mind similar to the one that created the poetry

- to create afresh the language and structure of the poem

Earle Birney, one of Canada's finest writers, once said:

> *'The essentials of poetry are rhythm, dance, and the human voice.'*

In his *Notes on the Art of Poetry* (1953), **Dylan Thomas** mused:

'I could never have dreamt that there were such goings-on in the world between the covers of books, such sandstorms and ice blasts of words . . . . . such staggering peace, such enormous laughter, such and so many blinding bright lights . . . . . splashing all over the pages in a million bits and pieces all of which were words, words, words, and each of which was alive forever in its own delight and glory and oddity and light.'

As a speaker you must always relish poetry. It is, after all, relished language.

PROSE SPEAKING

'Good Heavens! I am speaking prose! I have always spoken prose! I have spoken prose throughout my whole life!'

Moliere

This famous declaration, made by Monsieur Jourdain in the play *Le Bourgeois Gentilhomme,* clearly points to the importance of good prose speaking skills. Prose is the **everyday mode of language** all of us speak throughout our lives. Methodically practising effective delivery of different kinds of prose will enable speakers to communicate in richer and more versatile ways.

Most people have much more varied and interesting minds than their speaking indicates. The best prose speaking shows a complete fusion of intention and utterance – the talk hitting the listener as vocal thought.

It is therefore not surprising that examiners usually look at the author's intention and style when evaluating prose speaking. The extract should be understood and appreciated, phrasing and pause should assist the pointing of the meaning, and there should be a good use of modulation to make the passage lively and interesting. Also, examiners expect firm articulation from the presenter – to transmit the clarity of thought.

Q How can a teacher encourage a student to achieve all these things?

When students are very young

> **No technical points should be stressed.** Instead ask for understanding and enjoyment. Look for a sense of fun, pleasure or mystery, and encourage their involvement to be conveyed by facial expression. Indirectly they will be learning pace control, pause and application of characterization.

> **Always use extracts from a books below their own reading ability** – material they can easily relate to and have enjoyed in the past.

> **Consider choosing narrative and one or two characters.** Dialogue is much easier to learn because it encourages the imagination and solo characterization. Passages that contain a narrator and one/two characters can be found in fairy tales such as *Red Riding Hood:* (i) Wolf (ii) Narrator; folk tales such as *The Porridge Pot:* (I) Mother (ii) Daughter (iii) Narrator; **Roald Dahl** stories such as *The Enormous Crocodile* and *Fantastic Mr. Fox.* Divide a group into twos or threes – one to tell

the story and the others to be the characters.

➢ **Work on the characterization** by using a special voice – use pitch change and perhaps a feeling of dialect (maybe a country flavour with plenty of country sounds, or a local accent). Add gesture and movement if it helps. Body language will often assist in character creation and should be encouraged in the early stages.

➢ **Then work on the narrative** so that it paints a picture and develops atmosphere. There is often a tendency to rush the actual storytelling or to speak it in a monotone. Some students will have listened to audiotapes or the radio and will try to copy this 'broadcasting' style but they should remember that these speakers and readers have adapted their delivery to the medium they are working in. A live performance should come 'off the page'. It should have vitality and enthusiasm.

➢ **Choose material containing sentences that are fairly simple**. Long and involved sentences require careful phrasing and children will often try to speak them in one breath.

TRY THIS EXERCISE: To aid phrasing control, count aloud from 1 to 20 pausing after every 4 counts and taking a snatched breath through the mouth. Then find a sentence that can be divided into short phrases and practise saying it.

e.g. I went down to the shops today / because I was told by Sarah / that I could buy some new jeans / for only £5!

e.g. My dog ran away / but I found him later / looking very sad and miserable.

Concentrate on controlled pace and an easy natural intake of breath.

- **Increase the number of the group to three, four or five** – by adding extra characters to the passage. This could prove an interesting approach for a concert or presentation. Costume and props could add to the appreciation of the selection, and you could encourage creativity with make-up.

- **If you are working with a large group consider splitting it into sub-groups of four** – to give each student a chance to perform. Then allow the class time for discussion on how each group approached

33

the passage. Alternatively, different pages could be given to each group, so that the story develops and builds to its completion. This aids listening as well as speaking skills. Ask the performers if they thought they could improve their presentation.

➢ **NEVER criticize performers**. Always agree with their evaluation and add to it. If they can't see anything wrong with a performance, ask them to consider the pace of it. Was it good for the listeners? Might it have been better a little slower? This will encourage them to listen to their own work as well as other sub-groups.

➢ **Initially all the work should be read** – then phrasing can be planned and key words underlined.

Prose speaking from memory

This is often required in examinations. Sometimes the choice is a free one but certain examination boards set specific prose extracts.

The choice is extremely important:

- ➤ **It should always be within the student's capabilities and understanding**.

- ➤ **It should always contrast with the other selections.**

- ➤ **Always consider the length of the chosen extract** – the longer the candidate continues, the more likely s/he is to make mistakes. If the examination time limit is three minutes, then choose an extract of no more than 1½ - 2 minutes. Allow the extra time for an introduction to the selection.

- ➤ **Ask the students to choose passages for themselves** – with some narration and one or two characters if possible. Encourage the use of voices. Let each student read the chosen passage to the group or a partner.

ASK:

Q Was it fun?

Q Did the speaker enjoy it?

Q Did the audience enjoy it?

Q What about audibility?

Q Characterization?

Q Pause?

Q Did the narrative add to the presentation?

Eventually students must think about learning the prose passage off by heart. This can be done by constant reading of the extract and looking up at the audience. However, setting any child a large amount to learn by heart can be discouraging. When rehearsing, think about setting two or three sentences to practise reading aloud. Ask them to repeat it without the book the next lesson. If they can remember it well, they can move on to the next section. If not, let them do it once again with the book but this time discuss the meaning with them and encourage them to look at the key words. Ask what they can see when they read the story – help them to use their imagination. This is a slow process but through it they are setting the groundwork for their later studies.

Q What about the position of the speaker?

Some teachers like to place a character looking diagonally forward, with the narrator looking at the audience. This could be tried whilst reading so that a pattern is established. Ensure that the head turn is no more than 30 to 40 degrees – too sharp a movement can mean the loss of facial expression and vocal power.

Good basic breath support, projection, clarity and fluency of thought are always required but **imagination is the key to good prose speaking.**

When using eye contact, consider whether or not the extract is being shared with the whole audience. Endeavour to share the narrative rather than the characters' spoken words. If students find it difficult to use eye contact without losing concentration, ask them to think about looking at the audience's 'hair line': as this creates the impression of eye contact without eye-to-eye confrontation.

If you have a large group

Let them read to one another in twos, or divide into fours for group reading sessions. Encourage listening whilst other things are happening in the room – this aids

37

concentration. As a teacher it is sometimes possible to wander around the groups and then choose three or four students to perform for the whole class.

NOTE: These should be good examples in order to encourage the students to imitate the high standards achieved.

Mature students

Although mature students require a different approach, they need to develop the same techniques. Always think carefully about the type of text and the author's style when speaking prose.

⇨ ASK:

Q Is it mystery, horror, suspense, a family story, romance?

Q Is it designed to be story-telling, persuasion, reflective, hard-hitting or funny?

When choosing an extract to learn by heart, try NOT to have more than the narrator and two other characters. Unless the speaker is very skilled it will be very difficult to communicate more than three 'voices' effectively.

Mature candidates should consider **reading to children**. Use prepared reading as a method of learning the necessary skills. Create atmosphere, characters and use plenty of word colour. Make the extract full of vitality and enthusiasm. Think carefully about pace, pause, phrasing, tone colour and emphasis.

Most important of all, however, is look at the children. If they are NOT interested they will walk away!

If the book is very simple the pictures can be held facing the children and the story shared with items of interest pointed out.

By reading to very young children, confidence develops. The age level can then be lifted with books such as: *Magic Finger* by **Roald Dahl**; *The Worst Witch* by **Jill Murphy**; *Ace* and *Fox Busters* by **Dick King Smith**.

Progress to children's classics and read as if for a television programme looking forward at the camera with books such as: *The Secret Garden* by **Frances Hodgson Burnett**; *Alice in Wonderland* by **Lewis Carroll**; *Anne of Green Gables* by **L M Montgomery**; *The Railway Children* by **E Nesbit**; and *Huckleberry Finn* by **Mark Twain**.

Additional suitable books and authors

 YOUNGER STUDENTS

Books include: *The Fudge books, Tales of a 4th Grade Nothing and other stories* by **Judy Blume;** *Animal Ark* series by **Lucy Daniels;** *My Naughty Little Sister* by **Dorothy Edwards;** *Wind in the Willows* by **Kenneth Grahame;** *The Iron Man, Iron Woman* and *How the Whale Became* by **Ted Hughes;** *Kipper* by **Mike Inkpen;** the *Narnia* series by **C S Lewis;** *The Worst Witch* series by **Jill Murphy;** *The Magic Pudding* by **Norman Lindsey;** *The Belfry Witches, Broomsticks in Space* and *Witch You Were Here* by **Katie Saunders;** *The Silver Sword* and *There's No Escape* by **Ian Serraillier;** *The Owl Who Was Afraid of the Dark* by **Jill Tomlinson;** *The Twins* and *Mum Minder* by **Jacqueline Wilson.**

Authors include: **Michael Bond, Helen Cresswell, Roald Dahl, Michelle Magorian, A A Milne, Michael Morpugo, Beatrix Potter, Dick King Smith, Alison Uttley.**

NOTE: Books by **Paul Jennings** are particularly good for the 10 – 13 year age range as the sentences are short and the stories are amusing.

 *TEENAGERS*

Books include: *The Demon Headmaster* and *Revenge of the Demon Headmaster* by **Gillian Cross;** *Roll over Roly, Charm School* and *Goggle Eyes* by **Anne Fine;** *The Tin Princess, The Shadows in the North* and *The Tiger in the Well* by **Philip Pullman;** and *Castaway of the Flying Dutchmen* by **Brian Jacques.**

Authors include: **Terry Pratchett, J K Rowling** and other similar current writers, the classic works of **Sir Arthur Conan Doyle, Robert Louis Stevenson** and **Jules Verne.**

ADVANCED STUDENTS

Authors include: **Alan Bennett, Anne, Charlotte** and **Emily Brontë, Agatha Christie, Joseph Conrad, Charles Dickens, E M Forster, Paul Gallico, Grahame Greene, Laurie Lee, Daphne du Maurier, Frank McCourt, George Orwell, Ellis Peters, Ruth Rendall** and **Oscar Wilde**.

In addition: Look at books that are set for school examinations.

5   IMPROVISATION

'Improvisation is of enormous importance in the process of training and also of performance'

Lee Strasberg

Q What is improvisation?

Some people are quite fearful of the process, believing there to be something mysterious or unfathomable about it. To **improvise** is simply to **invent** or **create** and all of us do this throughout our lives. Whenever you get an idea, or fantasize, or dream, you are improvising – whether or not you remember that particular dream you had last night, you were certainly improvising while you were dreaming it! Invention or improvisation is absolutely essential when engaging in any form of drama.

When one of the greatest actors of the last century, Sir Ralph Richardson, was asked, *'What is acting?'* He immediate replied, *"It's dreaming – to order"*. And when one of the greatest actors of the 20th century, Juliette Stevenson, was asked what was the most important skill for the actor, she might have replied, *'my voice'*, *'my movement'* or *'my speech'* – but she didn't. Her answer was: *"My imagination"*.

The audience is fascinated by what is going on in your head; your thinking, your voice, your movement and your speech are essential means for conveying what is in your head – otherwise your mind would remain private, silent and invisible.

However, the physical means are not interesting in themselves. Unless you can adopt the author's thinking as your own – and in drama, the character's state of mind as your very own, you will not be able to convey anything of real worth. In consequence, **imagination and improvisation are absolutely essential.**

Improvisation is something all of us did at an extremely early age. Notice how bricks become actual animals in a zoo – transformed by a child's imagination or see how easily a child turns the bedroom into a shop – a real shop, more real than the bedroom itself.

Fine actors are people who have carefully nurtured this natural creative ability: they refuse to allow the business of growing up to rob them of such a precious resource.

Albert Einstein, the great physicist (who developed the special and general theories of relativity, the equivalence of mass and energy, and the photon theory of light!) once said of himself:

> *'I am enough of an artist to draw freely upon my imagination. Imagination is more important than knowledge. Knowledge is limited. Imagination encircles the world.'*

Young children love to play make believe – and dramatic improvisation is a natural progression from this. One child will often spontaneously lead others through a strange world of monsters, treasure maps and magic carpets. **Deliberately staged improvisation**, however, is usually something that requires greater confidence and flair.

Q How can we foster these qualities as we help our students to create and develop improvised dramatic situations?

Consider using mime as a stepping-stone.

TRY THIS: First of all get the students to perform hand exercises to stretch and limber up the fingers; ask them to pick up a variety of imaginary objects and consider their shape, size, and weight – do make sure that they always remember to put something down after they have picked it up!

Mime cleaning out a pet rabbit's cage, for example. Consider: The shape of the door/s, the weight of the animal and where to place the rabbit whilst cleaning the hutch. Clean out the hutch and replace the bedding, provide fresh food and water and place the rabbit back in the cage – or has it escaped? Ask the students to show all reaction with the face and with body language.

Repeat the mime, speaking thoughts aloud. Talk to the rabbit, and maybe ask an imaginary person where fresh food can be found.

Try performing the mime and the following improvisation in a group situation. Ask each child to perform as an individual and speak as loudly and clearly as possible. Children will gain a sense of security in a group situation when they feel there is no audience watching until they develop individual confidence. Encourage the mime to have shape by asking: Where are you? What happens? How does it end? This will give the students a firm basis for future improvisations.

➡️ OTHER IDEAS: Taking a dog for a walk, cleaning out a cupboard and finding a large spider or a mouse, making a sandwich, searching for a book, getting a drink for oneself and a friend or tidying up a bedroom while a cat or dog is present.

NOTE: Consider that it is often easier to create a scene whilst talking to a friend or an animal.

Reaction is always an important part of improvisation. We can react facially and / or verbally. Get students to work in twos, creating a story that needs reaction to a situation and to one another. Encourage strong emotions such as fear, horror and laughter. Then one of the pair can repeat his/her half of the improvised play individually imagining what the other is saying and doing.

➡️ POSSIBLE IMPROVISATION TITLES: Noises in the Night, The Sleepover or Lost in: . . . the Woods, . . . a Fog, . . . the Supermarket . . . or a Crowd.

When performing **solo improvisation** in an examination, candidates should try to make it short, sharp, and with a strong ending. Students should NEVER worry if examiners stop performances when they have seen enough of the candidates' imagination at work.

Improvisation and text

When a student has problems with a piece of text and the words are being said without depth of understanding or emotion, consider using improvisation to create similar meaning in a modern or familiar setting. Older students are capable of creating dialogue to communicate the ideas in a text although younger ones sometimes require assistance.

 TO HELP GREATER UNDERSTANDING: Take, for example, Viola's speech from **Shakespeare's** *Twelfth Night, Act 2 Scene 2 ('I left no ring with her . . . ')*. Modern language can be used, although not necessarily applied to each sentence. *'I didn't give her a ring – what's she talking about? I hope she hasn't fallen in love with me because of my disguise. She did stare at me – for a moment I thought she couldn't speak. And then she did – but in fits and starts. I think she loves me! How cunning of her to send that messenger. 'I don't want your Lord's ring'. He didn't send her one. It's me she loves!'*

Sometimes students find it difficult to do this with a complete speech. However, if students try it with small sections, they will find that it assists them to discover truth of meaning, mood and attitude. Then, as they acquire more awareness of the full meaning of text, they will employ richer vocal colour, intonation and rhythm when they return to the original text.

If it is the emotion that is weak, transfer the speech to a more familiar setting.

 TO HELP LACK OF EMOTION: Take, for example, the scene in *The Brontës* by **Alfred Sangster** where Charlotte has taken Emily's poems and read them. Ask students to create a scene where there are two sisters: one has taken the other's personal letters and is reading them aloud. Discuss how the first sister would feel on hearing her private letters read – how angry would she be! Ask the students how they would feel if these were their letters? Concentrate on the building up of genuine emotion.

Improvisation and characterization

To understand a character being presented in a solo scene or duologue, the student must first of all have:

- read the whole play

- make a note of the character's actions

- tried to analyse what sort of person s/he is.

The student should then experiment by creating an original scene, perhaps when the character was young, before the action of the play, or at a point in the future. Whilst this process is taking place, you might encourage the student to question, in character, actions and feelings, speaking the thoughts aloud. Invite the student to discuss, again in character, something in connection with what happens in the play with a friend or relation.

Improvisation will reveal the depth of knowledge regarding the whole play and the character's relationship with others. It provides invaluable assistance to the performer, boosting confidence through a much deeper knowledge and strengthening characterization.

NOTE: Incidentally, Trinity examiners sometimes request this type of related improvisation, so practice will improve spontaneity and confidence.

'Reading aloud teaches children about literature in a way that silent or independent reading never can.'

Judy Freeman

There are things that must be considered before any reading commences. The reader must think about stance, position of the book, position of the audience, size of the room and how much light is available.

> **Correct posture is important** – for breathing and projection. It also communicates confidence.

> **The book should be held** – in front of the body and in such a position that it does not hide the mouth otherwise it will hinder projection. The reader should be able to look at the page and the audience without moving their head – eye movement is all that is necessary. Any lowering of the chin squashes the larynx and also alters the flow of the vocal projection. Some students prefer to hold the book with two hands and this is quite acceptable, especially if the book is heavy. One hand can hold the spine base and the other can be placed at the side of the book where the section is to be read. This provides a link with the line or paragraph that is being communicated and assists students who fear they might lose their place. The

side hand can slide down the page as the reading progresses. If students are confident, they can hold the book with one hand and relax the other but they must always be ready to turn over the page.

➢ **Consider the light** – this should always fall on the page. If the room is in semi-darkness, allow time to adjust the eyes when looking back to the written word.

➢ **Always ensure that the audience can see the reader's face** – and when eye contact is used remember to look to one area rather than trying to sweep the eyes across the whole audience. The area can vary each time, especially if the audience is widely spread.

➢ **If the room is large** – it will be necessary to slow the pace and allow plenty of breath support for stronger projection.

Working with young children

Ensure that their reading aloud commences with their own choices – they will love to share something they have enjoyed. However, when preparing for examinations, you should guide them to select material well within their practical capabilities – explore, for example, a book the child read one or two years previously. Assist them to choose a passage that has some narrative and a little conversation (see 4 PROSE SPEAKING p.30). Try to find something that has a good strong or dramatic ending. Check that the passage is not too long – let them read to other children and if attention starts to wander then the passage needs to be cut.

When the extract has been selected, consider the following points:

> **When introducing the selection encourage the student is to look up all the time**. This is an important part of the complete reading because it communicates the book, author and setting. If an explanation of the extract is required it should be short and concise.

> **Make a copy of the passage and assist the student by underlining in pencil where to look up.** At first always make it towards the end of a sentence. However, if the sentence is too long let the student look up half way through.

> **Punctuation pauses should be observed.** Consider using numbers of <u>beats</u> (as in music), or road signs if the students are older, to convey the length of pause for punctuation.

For example:

- a comma = <u>one beat</u> or slow down sign

- a full stop = <u>a minim</u> or stop sign

- new paragraphs should have at least three beats = <u>a dotted minim</u> or traffic lights!

If students find this difficult at first, get them to tap out the beats with their foot or hand. Once control is gained, the reading can begin to be communicated clearly.

➤ **The phrasing can be marked in pencil** – if needed. Marking the page often assists readers to feel more confident. This confidence assists them to create atmosphere and characters.

➤ **When conversation occurs in a passage** – the student could try changing vocal pitch for the different voices. The student should establish eye contact with audience for the narrative and then perhaps look in different directions for each character.

> **To capture the mood** – encourage the student to experiment with change of pace.

> **To give the passage atmosphere** – encourage the varied use of power (loud and soft).

> **So the listener has time to tune in to the reader's voice** – encourage the student to commence slowly.

> **So that the audience is ready for the end** – the reader should usually slow down when coming to an end.

> **Beware learning the words off by heart** – as there is a great deal of difference between reading and speaking. Reference should always be made to the book and the words lifted off the page with vitality and enthusiasm.

Adults should be taught in exactly the same way with the book being marked and the basic pause and phrasing being observed.

Prepared reading is an excellent way to move on to sight-reading.

'Pleasant words are a honeycomb, sweet to the soul and healing to the bones.'

Solomon

Effective sight-reading depends largely upon quickness of mind. Time is very limited and the reader should therefore focus upon processes that can be accomplished quickly:

➤ **Look at the name of the book and the author** – Does this tell you anything? Sometimes you may recognize the author and have expectations about the style of writing.

➤ **Look at the first and last sentences** – so that a good beginning and ending can be made.

➤ **Quickly scan the passage for its overall flavour.**

➤ **Look for any long or unfamiliar words** – say them in the mind or shape them. If words are unknown, then try them.

- ➤ **Try not to speak anything at all until you have in mind a definite phrase** (a **piece of meaning**) – always remember that we communicate through speaking phrases, not by uttering individual words. If you mentally grasp a phrase before speaking it you are likely to give it colour.

- ➤ **Examiners do NOT mark word accuracy** – they award credit for how quickly you can communicate the main thrust of a passage. That's all any of us has time to do when we're sight-reading, however experienced we are! Remember that usually more than half the words in any given sentence are irrelevant to the core meaning of that sentence.

- ➤ **Try to look up at the ends of sentences.**

- ➤ **Control the pace.**

- ➤ **Use character voices where appropriate.**

- ➤ **Above all try to create atmosphere, directing everything to the listener** – NEVER forget that everything is being done for the listener.

- ➤ **Whatever you do, DON'T read to the page!**

'Acting is nothing more or less than playing. The idea is to humanize life.'

George Eliot

This interesting claim by Eliot points to the fact that **acting has a function**: to make some aspect of living more understandable. Some forms of acting are not audience related and are engaged in solely for the benefit of the actor/s. However, theatre acting should always share something about life with an audience. Prepared acting in Speech and Drama examinations should be very similar to theatre acting in that the focus should be on performing that speaks to an audience.

The Canadian actor **Kate Reid** went as far as saying that *'acting is not being emotional, but being able to express emotion'*. The finest actors learn to train and to control the most sensitive material available to any craftsman – the living organism of a human being in all of its manifestations (mental, physical, vocal and emotional). As an actor you are at once the instrumentalist and the instrument itself: your three-part instrument being your mind, your body and your voice.

A real person always has 3 Ps:

- a **P**ast

- a **P**resent

- a **P**otential

The same is true for the overwhelming majority of characters in drama. The script itself will give you some information but it will never provide you with all you need to know and understand: your imagination will be called upon to provide that. Think about your actual self, born in a particular place, raised in particular circumstances. You have developed particular tastes, preferences, beliefs and relationships. You have particular aspirations, desires, regrets and ambitions.

A Riddle:

What's the well-known 'abbreviation' that's actually three times as long as the unabbreviated phrase?

Answer:

www. That's nine syllables (dʌb lju dʌb lju dʌb lju), whereas *World Wide Web* has only three syllables (wɜld waid wɛb).

As a memory aid, **a mnemonic**, try expanding the famous *www* into *WWWW:* **4 Ws**! Now use **each of the 4 Ws** as the first letter of **4 crucial questions** you will always ask yourself when you are acting, regardless of what character you are playing:

Q **W**ho am I?

Q **W**here am I?

Q **W**hy am I here?

Q **W**hat do I want to happen?

These are questions you would have little or no difficulty answering if you were thinking about your real self. Make certain that the dramatic character you create has a similar substance, structure and credibility.

Every time you act a scene you must be:

> ➤ **Keenly aware of your different self.** Only very rarely is your full normal self completely apt for the character you are meant to play.
> (**W**ho am I?)

> **Keenly aware of the imagined location.** Hardly ever is the stage itself meant to be the context of the action. The stage should almost always be transported by your imagination into another place. *'On your imaginary forces work'* **William Shakespeare**.
(**W**here am I?)

> **Keenly aware of why you, the character, are in this imagined place at this time**. Did you arrive by parachute? Did someone force you here? Did you come here with enthusiasm?
(**W**hy am I here?)

> **Keenly aware of your intentions, ambitions, hopes, plans and strategies**. These desires will almost definitely be different from those of other characters in the play and this will give rise to the drama (drama = conflict). The play would be very bland indeed without dramatic conflict.
(**W**hat do I want to happen?)

Acting solo

Choice of scene and character are all-important – and should always be within the actor's capabilities. This is particularly important as far as children are concerned. A child should aim for a simple and natural performance with good pace control and use of pause. Above all the child must enjoy acting the scene and relate to the character.

Some monologues are spoken directly to the audience and these do not usually require detailed characterization, abundant imagination or a convincing use of the acting space. When performing such material, the actor should make the dialogue conversational and expressive while including plenty of lively facial expression. S/he should endeavour to move naturally with relaxed hands and only use gesture if it supports the dialogue or the personality of the speaker.

The performer must NEVER focus exclusively on the examiner. The speech should be delivered to an imaginary audience stretching beyond the examiner and to either side.

The actor should NEVER turn the head sharply at right angles to the examiner. Keep the movement to no more than thirty degrees.

NOTE: This 'direct speech' type of solo performance does not teach a student much about stagecraft and should not be used consistently.

Scenes are available in which students can use their **imagination** and act with a sense of **spontaneity**. Characters such as: Snow White, Red Riding Hood, Alice in Wonderland, Pinocchio or Charlie from **Roald Dahl's** *Charlie and the Chocolate Factory* [dramatized by **Richard R George**] all provide opportunities for young actors to experiment with speaking their thoughts aloud whilst imagining the situation and the setting.

The performer should NEVER be over-aware of the audience but should concentrate on seeing only the world created by the imagination.

After the initial reading and a discussion on the meaning of the words and the situation, **start setting the scene**. When children are quite young this will assist them to remember the words. Draw lines from the two back (upstage) corners of the stage towards the examiner so as to form a triangle and place any necessary furniture facing towards that triangle point in the audience. Try to avoid placing items of furniture in the middle of the stage because this will cut it in half and restrict movement. If the stage is large, ensure that younger children perform in front of the furniture as much as possible. Although the performer should attempt to use the stage effectively, s/he should only move if and when it is dictated by the thoughts and feelings of the character.

NOTE: The actor should NOT stand behind furniture unless it is essential to the play.

If a character is vocalizing thoughts, then make sure the student understands that eye contact with the audience should NOT normally be employed. If other characters are supposed to be present, ensure that they are imaginatively positioned on the stage and created by the performer's reactions and responses.

When students are a little older (10 – 13) they can begin to consider in more detail the **use of the body** – the movement, poise and gesture of characters.

Students should think carefully about deportment. If a king or queen is to be acted, for example, play the deportment game – balancing a book on the head and moving around an obstacle course of boxes and chairs. Ask girls to consider walking with a long dress, which means that the toes must lead the way – if they walk normally with heel and then toe, they will tread on the hem and rip the dress!

Practise sitting. Commence walking from the left back comer and move towards a chair placed right of centre, facing slightly diagonally towards the triangle point.

NOTE: The performer must NEVER look at the chair but should be aware of it.

Feel the chair with the side of the leg and then turn to face the front. Place one foot back under it like a curtsy. Lower into the chair using the thigh and stomach muscles so that at any point the movement could be halted. Keep the back very straight and the head erect.

When seated, place feet together and hands relaxed onto the lap. Imagine that the chair is a throne. When rising to leave, again place one foot under the chair and lift upwards. Never lean forward or the 'crown' will fall off! Place the feet together before moving. Remember to lead with the right foot when walking to the right, and the left foot when walking to the left.

Think about the type of person being created.

Q   Is s/he proud, cunning, scared or full of confidence?

Q   How does this affect the body language?

Improvisation and characterization

⇨ TRY THIS: To help students become aware of their characters' physical appearance, use mime. Walking about the room as a very proud person, notice how the head is held and how the nose lifts up! Then create a shy character whose head drops and who doesn't make eye contact - notice how such characters tend to curl inwards and that they usually walk with small steps.

Then create a number of different types appropriate to student age: anxious, fearful, confident, nosey, domineering, an alcoholic or compulsive eater. Give them certain jobs: a model, a reporter, a computer whiz, a teacher or a gym instructor. Let two of the characters meet – and mime their reactions and responses to one another. Finally place several of them together at a party and create an improvisation using appropriate spoken language. Remind the students that they must sustain a character's body language.

Consider how movement changes with age. Observe a child learning to walk, how it bounces as it gets a bit older; contrast this with a teenager, a busy housewife in a supermarket, a business man, a mature person visiting a library with time on their hands, or an older person with a walking stick.

⇨ TRY THIS: Mime the difference in body language for these people of different ages. Then let two of the people meet. Remember, as a person gets older s/he needs stability and the gap between the feet widens and then the knees bend slightly to give support, and when old, the head will tend to move forward to lead the way. Students should consider these tendencies when playing the part of an elderly person or a character such as a witch.

During dialogue, never bend from the waist because this causes the breathing apparatus to be squashed and voice projection becomes difficult.

Gesture should always support the character's emotions. It should never be repetitive, constant like a windmill or merely a movement from the elbow!

Students can develop confidence by practising the following 2 exercises:

⇨ CUTTING EXERCISE

The body has a central line running down from the head to the floor and at first the gesturing hand should not go across the imaginary line. Bend the arm at the elbow and place the hand at the height of the middle of the body. Cut the hand down and forward at an angle of 45 degrees, and at the same time look at the comer of the room. Relax the hand and let it move down to the side of the body. This can be repeated lifting the arm and elbow to chest level and cutting at the same angle so that the arm is about shoulder level. Again raise the elbow but leave the hand at the middle of the chest, then cut upwards towards the comer of the room just above the eye level.

This can be repeated with the other arm and the movement accompanied by words such as: *NO, WAIT, STOP* and *GO*. The hand position can be altered to suit the word (for example, *GO* – one finger pointing; *STOP* – the palm raised).

The exercise can be done with two hands. When this is done the wrists cross and the hands move over the central line. Stronger words can be used such as: *NEVER, HALT, AWAY.*

After the strong cut, it is useful to relax the arm down to the side, which maintains the condition of strength. If the hand is curled in and the arm drawn back to the body, a weak or indecisive character is created.

This exercise teaches students to move the arms with confidence.

GENTLE REFERENTIAL GESTURE EXERCISE

Again be aware of the imaginary central line. This time the back of the hand moves into the centre of the body with the arm fully relaxed. On reaching the line, the hand and arm are lifted a little and moved in a circle out to the 45 degree position with the palm uppermost. The arm is then relaxed to the side.

This can be repeated at chest level, and from the chest swinging the arm up and out to the high position. Phrases can be employed such as: *IT'S THERE, LOOK AT THE FIELDS, LOOK AT THE TREES* and *SEE THE SKY?* Remember the hands go up in front, complete the movement to the position and then circle out and down.

When using both arms, the hands should NEVER meet in the middle – there should always be a small gap between them.

This exercise assists in the development of gentle arm movement.

Before a scene is staged decide who else is on stage.

➪ ASK:

Q Where are they?

Q Are they sitting or standing? (watch the eye levels)

Try to place others downstage if possible so that the audience can see all facial expression.

NEVER place other characters in the audience or look at the examiner as if s/he is another character. Remember the audience is not part of the stage.

As solo scenes for examinations are often performed in a room, consider placing a gap between the examiner and the imagined front of the stage.

Teach young students to perform in a proscenium arch setting so that they learn the basic rules of stagecraft i.e. awareness of sight lines, commencing walking with the correct foot, not speaking with their backs to the audience, etc. It is important to learn these basic rules. Then when students acquire sufficient vocal and physical control they will have the ability to break the rules effectively where appropriate.

Older students must always be familiar with the full play and how their characters relate to others. The older a student, the more the character should be studied in depth and a psychological profile prepared. The scene should be considered line by line and each thought and reaction noted.

If there is no other character on stage, decide why words are said.

 ASK:

Q What does the character really mean?

Q What is s/he thinking and feeling?

Use pause to show changes of thought, and allow time for the thought process to be communicated.

Cut subsidiary characters for examination purposes. It is usually permissible to cut or imagine their utterance – as long as this kind of editing does not sacrifice the meaning and clarity of the scene. If one or more other characters are meant to be on stage, pause MUST be used before responding and reacting facially to what is heard or seen. However, the full time for the other character/s to speak cannot be allowed, otherwise the flow of the scene would be unduly interrupted. Allow just two or three seconds while maintaining concentration on the behaviour and words of any imagined character/s.

Consider the movement once a full appreciation of the dialogue has been acquired. To assist older students, let them read a speech aloud while walking about the room, moving in different ways and directions when thoughts or mood change. This makes them more aware of the underlying thought patterns. Encourage older students to stage their scenes and discuss the resulting physical patterns. Invite them to think about the type of character when moving. Is s/he honest, confident and straightforward? If so, s/he will probably move in direct lines. Characters that are devious, cunning, nervous or unstable will more likely walk in curves, circles and/or use angles. Students should NEVER continually repeat the same movement pattern. Vary the shape of the scene.

Constantly consider the audience who need always to relate to the character. A static scene can become boring after a while, unless the speaker has excellent vocal technique and detailed flexibility, sensitivity and intensity. Remember that movement can communicate underlying tension or emotional motivation.

Think carefully about period and costume – as this will affect deportment, movement and gesture. Some costumes prevent arms being lifted too high and stop a character from turning quickly. ALWAYS think about the undergarments and the shoes. There is also the use of the fan and handkerchief to consider. All these aspects require extra research and depth of appreciation.

The style of the writing should be very carefully considered.

⇨ ASK:

Q What type of play is it?

Q What effect should it have on an audience?

Q How is the language written?

Q Is verse form employed?

Q If so, why?

Think about style. Comedy should usually be played with a light touch and move at a fair pace, farce is even quicker with strong punch lines. Melodrama needs a marked dramatic awareness, strong gesture and a touch of over-reaction. Try always to appreciate what the writer is communicating, through use of language and character relationships.

Voice can be a powerful means of showing a character through its actual quality, and also through use of inflection, intonation and emphasis. Beware of straining the vocal cords, forcing the sound, shouting or tensing the throat and shoulders. Every performance should commence with a relaxation exercise to aid the ability to achieve breath support and to focus on the character and atmosphere to be created (see VI *RELAXATION* p.122).

Much depends on the ability of the student – so choose material carefully. Let them extend themselves and try different styles for practice but use their most effective characterizations for examination purposes.

Throughout the planning and monitoring of their work as actors, **students should constantly ask themselves these fundamental questions**:

Q Do I understand the character and situation as described by the play?

Q Am I conveying the character and situation as described by the play?

Q Have I applied sufficient depth of thought and
   imagination?

Q Is my characterization convincingly defined?

Q Do I need to improvise more?

Q Are my stylistic choices apt?

Q Are my stylistic choices persuasively realized?

Q Is my voice well supported and tonally
   unobstructed?

Q Am I employing apt and varied use of my voice
   and speech?

Q Am I employing apt and varied use of
   movement and use of space?

Q Is my performance suitably projected?

Q Is my performance designed for the full benefit
   of the audience?

Q Am I able to create and live an imagined
   situation?

Q Is my concentration sustained?

Q Is there continuous creative invention?

Q Is there continuous attention to detail?

Q Is there appropriate character interaction?

Q Is the dramatic situation being clearly
   established?

Q Is the performance space being used well?

Q Do I give the impression that all my behaviour,
   i.e. all movement and vocalization, stems from
   situation and / or character rather than from
   learning and rehearsal?

Suitable authors

 YOUNGER AND INTERMEDIATE STUDENTS

Adaptations by: **Alfred Bradley, David Conville, Neil Duffield, Carol Anny Duffy, David Gooderson, Bill Gavin, John Hartoch, Frank Lowe, Pete Meakin, Mary Morris, Susan Nanus, Ron Nicol, Peter Oswald, Caroline Reader, Glyn Robbins, Dave Simpson, Tim Supple, Jules Tasca, Paul Thain** and **David Wood.**

Authors include: **Alan Ayckbourn, Edna Baker, J M Barrie, Tony Barton, Richard Blythe, Robert Bolt, Alfred Bradley, Bertolt Brecht, Ken Campbell, David Clarke, Denise Coffey, Fiz Coleman, Colin and Mary Crowther, Alan Cullen, Georgia Dobbs, Ellen Dryden, Les Ellison, David Foxton, John Gardiner, Jamila Gavin, Bernard Goss, Nicholas Stuart Gray, Noël Greig, Willis Hall, Margaret Harding, Sebastian Hayes, Graham Holliday, David Holman, Tony Horitz, Graham Jones, Randall Lewton, Sharman MacDonald, Wes Magee, Blanche Marvin, A A Milne, Dilys Owen, Brian Patten, V A Pearn, Saviour Pirotta, Phil Porter, Shaun Prendergast, Peter Richards, Philip Ridley, Belinda Roberts, David E. Rowley, Willy Russell, Noël Scott, Dodie Smith, Paul Thompson, Bill Tordoff, Richard Tydeman, Nick Warburton, Brian Way, Ken Whitmore, John Wiles, David Henry Wilson, Patricia Wood** and **Carol Younghusband.**

ADVANCED STUDENTS

Authors include: **Jean Anouilh, John Arden,** Aristophanes, Alan Ayckbourn, Hilary Beaton, Samuel Beckett, Brendan Behan, Aphra Behn, Edward Bond, Bertolt Brecht, Howard Brenton, Anton Chekhov, Caryl Churchill, William Congreve, Noël Coward, T S Eliot, Nick Enright, Euripides, George Farquhar, Dario Fo, David French, Brian Friel, Athol Fugard, Pam Gems, Michael Gow, Roger Hall, David Hare, Tony Harrison, Henrik Ibsen, Eugène Ionesco, Ray Lawler, Sharman MacDonald, David Mamet, Christopher Marlowe, Arthur Miller, Sean O'Casey, Eugene O'Neill, John Osborne, Louise Page, Arthur Wing Pinero, Harold Pinter, Luigi Pirandello, Franca Rame, Terence Rattigan, James Reaney, Willy Russell, William Shakespeare, George Bernard Shaw, Sam Shepard, R B Sheridan, Sophocles, Wole Soyinka, August Strindberg, J M Synge, Sue Townsend, Michelene Wandor, Timberlake Wertenbaker, Arnold Wesker, Oscar Wilde, Emlyn Williams, Tennessee Williams and David Williamson.

9   CHORAL SPEAKING

'Choral Speech refers to a group speaking and interpreting as a choir.'

Calgary Kiwanis Music Festival

Teachers who have tried **choral speaking** almost invariably appreciate the benefits. Whether you have only two pupils or twenty, we would urge you to introduce them to the hugely enjoyable process of combined speaking. All students benefit because they can all be involved and it does not matter whether they have a great deal of experience or none at all. The teacher can develop not only their speaking and listening skills but also their performing disciplines through this one medium. Shy children gain confidence and learn teamwork. All children gain an appreciation of rhythm and develop their imaginative and artistic skills. Vocal work is inevitably improved because clarity is all-important, and variations of pitch, pace, pause, power, inflection, tone and stress are all involved when students are engaged in choral work.

Before the choice of poetry is made the teacher must consider how to approach the creating of a choir.

Try to balance the choir by dividing them into groups of similar voices. Using a very short poem or nursery rhyme that can be learnt off by heart, ask each individual to speak the verse aloud. Decide whether the speaker has a high, middle or low range – is the voice light, medium or heavy? Then place him/her in the appropriate group. When teaching primary children, remember that their voices will have little variation in pitch. However they will have light or strong voices and individuality, which can be used to good effect. The teacher who knows the abilities of the children can almost immediately place them into suitable groups. If, however, the class is a new one and familiarity has yet to be established, let the group speak as a whole without any division. Concentrate on speaking 'as one' and this will aid the students with their listening and timing.

⇨ THINK ABOUT: **Stance.** Always commence a class with some form of relaxation exercise and posture awareness (see VI *RELAXATION* p.122). Teach the group to present a confident picture.

⇨ THINK ABOUT: **Shape**. A visual effect is important. Beginners standing together feel the support of one another.

Consider:

> **Triangles** – either with the base line at the back and the line to the front gradually lowering so that the point speakers are sitting on two knees; or with

the base line in the front with all the students seated rising to a point at the centre back using the taller students.

> A **square** grouping can communicate a look of strength providing that the children rise in height so that every face is visible.

> **Semi-circles** are attractive and sometimes boxes or steps can be used to give height variation.

> **Rectangles** can be achieved by using the point of one corner towards the audience. If the poem is to have movement or characterization. Consider placing the group to one side on the diagonal line so they can be seen and also view the acting themselves.

➡ Having chosen the choir and taught them how to stand, the teacher must then make these **4 key decisions:**

1   **Choice of material**

2   **How the material is to be presented**

3   **How to achieve clarity**

4   **Whether the teacher will conduct the choir or allow them to control themselves**

Choose material according to age range

Younger children are better with shorter poems that teach them togetherness and rhythmic appreciation.

 Suitable pieces include: *The Flower Seller* by **Eleanor Farjeon**; *The Small Ghostie* by **Barbara Ireson**; *The Band Passes* by **P King**; *The Sea* by **John Kitching**; *The Digging Song* and *The Witch's Brew* by **Wes Magee**; *Grannys Boot* by **Spike Milligan**; *A Busy Day* by **Michael Rosen**; *Windy Nights* by **R L Stevenson**.

Children can use the occasional gesture to support or accent a poem's dramatic language when they reach 10 – 11. However, too many gestures will create 'individuals' and the timing will not be sharp. It will also mean the children think too much about the gestures and getting them right, rather than communicating the words.

 Suitable pieces include: *The Dolphin and The Hiccup* by **Alan Bold**; *The Alleyway* by **Richard Edwards**; *Miss Tarrent* by **Gregory Harrison**; *Hallowe'en* by **Jean Kenward**; *The Owl and the Pussycat* by **Edward Lear**; *Up on the Downs, Jumping Jack and a Short Cut - After Dark* by **Wes Magee**; *We've Got a Wa Wa* by **Ropy Robinson** and *The Sick Young Dragon* by **Derek Stuart**. Suitable poets include **Katharine Blowen** and **Robin Klein**.

As the work progresses and the ability of the choir develops, consideration can be given to using individual speakers for certain lines or characters. Depending on the type of poem, a character can be created with mime and costume, or the individual can actually speak the words. Remember that this is CHORAL work and the choir must speak the bulk of the narrative. DON'T let the characters take over so that a play is performed. Maintain a feeling of group speaking but ensure variety.

Teenagers appreciate stories to dramatize and enjoy experimenting with language. At this age dance/drama is often possible and if you have students who move freely do consider this form of work.

 Suitable pieces include: *Matilda, George, Rebecca* and *Henry King* by **Hilaire Belloc;** *Jabberwocky* by **Lewis Carroll;** *Our Day in Perranporth Pet Shop* and *The Ballad of the Bread-man* by **Charles Causle;** *Sing in the Streets* by **Leonard Clark;** *Revolting Rhymes* and *Dirty Beasts* by **Roald Dahl;** *Albert and the Lion, The Return of Albert* and *The Battle of Hastings* by **Marriott Edgar;** *Old Possum's Book of Practical Cats* by **T S Eliot;** *The Jumblies* and *The Pobble Who Had No Toes* by **Edward Lear;** *The House on the Hill* and *Big Aunt Flo* by **Wes Magee;** *Just Another Day* by **Roger McGough;** *Grim and Gloomy* by **James Reeves.**

Older students can choose themes and collect poetry related to them or even write their own material. A mixture of poetry and prose could be linked together. This will be suitably challenging for the students and expand their awareness. Consider themes such as: *School, Bullying, Pollution, Nature, Animals, the Seasons, Space* and *Travel.*

 Try extracts from longer narratives such as: *The Pied Piper* by **Robert Browning;** *Hiawatha* by **Henry Wadsworth Longfellow;** *The Highwayman* by **Alfred Noyes;** *The Man from Snowy River and Other Ballads* by **Banjo Patterson;** *Goblin Market* by **Christina Rossetti;** *The Cremation of Sam McGrew* by **Robert W Service;** *The Lady of Shalott* by **Alfred, Lord Tennyson** and some of the poems of **Henry Lawson.**

Mature students might also experiment with antiphonal work – in poetry such as *Drake's Drum* by **Sir Henry Newbolt** or *Psalms* from the *Holy Bible.*

Adults can vary their choices by using verse plays such as those by **T S Eliot**, **Christopher Fry** and the ancient Greek playwrights. Try ballads of various countries, narratives, odes and humorous selections.

Performances can often be prepared for special audiences. Sometimes they can relate to recent moral issues or occurrences that have been reported in the newspapers and other media.

Think about the presentation of material

Discuss the poem with the students and ensure they understand every word and are aware of processes such as **enjambment** (see III *PAUSING* p.118). Make sure they are aware of the importance of bringing out humour, building up to climaxes and how **alliteration** (see XVI *USEFUL DEFINITIONS* p.169) may be used for effect. The teacher must make the final decisions about pauses, pace, other details and the overall effect.

Ensure clarity

Work on articulation exercises, encouraging the use of final consonants. Always provide separate exercises to improve speech – NEVER the performance poem itself. Students should be constantly encouraged to correct faults in the speaking of a poem and listen to the sounds they are making. Speech should be formed with firm attack but make sure it is also flexible – the performance should never become laboured. Endeavour to maintain an impression of spontaneity, being careful not to over-rehearse the work. If the poem is to be used for a special date, work towards that time and then put the poem aside. Bring it out two weeks before the event and polish it.

Let the students enjoy their work and share their pleasure with the audience.

Conducting

When they begin their work in choral speaking, children will need to be encouraged and conducted so that they are speaking together. Then, as their confidence increases the teacher can aid them by stepping aside. The performance will then be all their own. Practise their introduction to the poem – pausing for two counts, inhaling and speaking. As the students learn pause and timing they will gradually be in tune with one another and their work will improve.

If you do not have a group of children – and have as few as **two students**, DO consider using choral work. A short programme can be created using poems and stories linked to a theme. Try using one choral poem and then an individual poem for each child. **T S Eliot's** *Old Possum's Book of Practical Cats* can be very popular with students. Then, for example, the one listening could sit on the floor holding a toy cat. There are many poems suitable for individual and choral speaking. With two students it is easy to incorporate movement and gesture – use boxes or chairs for sitting at different levels, small props or costume accessories, photo frames, books, hats and cloaks, etc.

 There are several useful books on the subject if you wish to develop your own skills in this field. Try any of the following: *Fun with Choral Speaking* by **R M Anthony;** *The Speech Choir: With American Poetry* and *English Ballads for Choral Reading* by **Marjorie Gullan;**

Speech Improvement Through Choral Speaking by **Elizabeth E Keepie;** *Choral Speaking and the Verse Choir* by **E Kingsley Povenmire** and *Many Voices: A Collection of Poems Suitable for Choral Speech* by **Mona Swann.**

Choral speaking can be great fun. Even if it is never used for examination work, choral speaking can breed confidence and broaden knowledge and ability.

Choral prose speaking

Much of the choral speaking advice given is applicable when speaking prose.

Try using extracts with shorter sentences for young children. Find a mixture of direct speech and narrative. Several children could speak the words of one character when making an early attempt at group speaking. As there is no rhythmical stress, the students have to appreciate timing and length of pauses. Phrasing is essential, and teachers will need to conduct the choir at first in order to keep them all together.

Always consider shapes for the positioning of the choir. For prose speaking the group can often be divided into two or three sections – perhaps a central group for the narrative base and the side groups for direct speech. Experiment with shapes that assist the atmosphere of the chosen piece.

Think about the drama within the extract. Use plenty of changes of volume and DON'T be afraid to include whispering. Although group prose speaking is NOT easily accomplished, it usually adds to the students' enjoyment and teaches them vocal expression and pace control.

 Some suitable material: *The Iron Man, The Iron Woman* (these have a lovely mixture of noises!) and *How the Whale Became and Other Stories* by **Ted Hughes**; A House Inside Out (which has pleasing mixture of conversation and narrative) by **Penelope Lively**; any popular fiction such as **J K Rowling's** *Harry Potter series*, the *Narnia* tales by **C S Lewis** and other classics such as **J R Tolkein's** *The Hobbit* and *Lord of the Rings*.

10   PREPARED TALKS

'The passions are the only orators which always persuade.'

Francois de La Rouchefoucauld

Young students can be taught to communicate information, ideas, opinions and feelings through the simple medium of spoken communication. Initially the student can bring an object and say how and when s/he obtained it, show a book and describe the story or provide a photo and talk about when and where it was taken. On the other hand, s/he might prefer to explain how to play a game of cards, a board game, or how to make something. There are so many options regarding subject matter and it is very important that children choose topics that appeal to them. This will enable them to develop ease of fluency and confidence before they are asked to give a complete prepared talk.

Then later, when advising students on the choice of subject for a talk or presentation, try to guide them to something that appeals to them and with which they are familiar. Students can then research and investigate less familiar topics for their subject matter as they progress and gain confidence in their ability to speak in an uninterrupted way.

Always ask how much they know about whatever title they choose.

Ask the student to draw a circle and place the subject of the talk in the centre. Then 'brainstorm' around the circle, writing down everything s/he can possibly think of that is related to the subject. Use spider legs to link the items to the subject.

Let us take the subject of MUSIC as an example. The spider diagram might develop into something like this:

SPIDER DIAGRAM

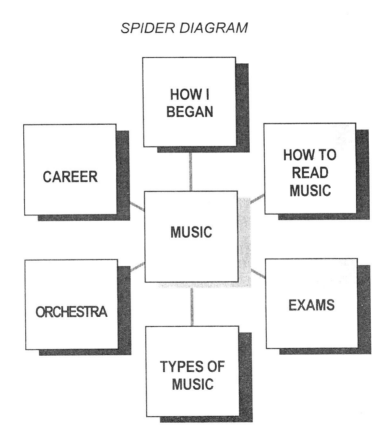

Decide on the aim of the talk – this is MOST important and then perhaps a specific title. Look at the subsections on the 'spider' and number them in a logical order using only those that relate to the aim. If there are more than four consider which are the most important.

Plan the sections of the talk.

1:	Introduction
2, 3 and 4:	Sections as chosen
5:	Conclusion

The introduction needs thinking about very carefully. A good beginning is highly important and catches the audience's attention. Try not to say, *"I am going to talk to you about . . . . ."* **Gordon Luck** in his book *Guide to Practical Speech Training* (see FURTHER READING) suggests some interesting ways of introducing a talk that you may find useful.

The following various ways of introducing a talk relate to the subject of MUSIC:

> ➤ **A list:** *"Violin, viola, cello, double bass are all stringed instruments that can be found in an orchestra. Today I would like to tell you how I became interested in playing the violin and how it has introduced me to a wide variety of music".*

> **a remembered incident**: *"Who would like to join the school orchestra?" Miss Gilpin said one day in assembly. She then went on to explain that if we went to the hall during the lunch period we could try the instruments and see if we were interested in learning to play one. I went along and formed an attachment to a double bass!"*

> **a link with the audience**: *"When you were at school did you ever get the opportunity to play an instrument? I did, and for the past three years I have been having lessons on how to play the trumpet."*

> **a startling statement**: *"'Cats yowling!' That's what my father said when I told him I had taken up the violin."*

> **a noise**: Either play a tape recording of a first class instrumentalist or alternatively bang two cymbals together. *"That's quite a noise . . . . . Not all instruments in an orchestra are so loud."*

Choose an introduction that suits the talk and practise delivering it confidently.

The conclusion can be related back to the opening so that the talk is neatly rounded off.

For example, *"My Father no longer thinks of violin music as 'Cats yowling' and I believe he quite enjoys listening to the school orchestra!"*

Visual aids

A prepared talk provides the opportunity for the speaker to use **visual aids** in the form of leaflets, posters, objects, utensils, flip charts, overhead projectors, videos or computer links.

The word '**presentation**' is often used to describe an act of public speaking that includes presented illustrative material. The supporting material is usually of a visual kind. However, other forms of illustration are sometimes used including recorded or live music, spoken material, dramatic work, audience participation and processes involving other audience senses such as taste, touch, and sometimes even smell!

Ensure that visual aids do not overwhelm the viewer but add to the information provided. It is far better to have a few items on display, which can be referred to in the presentation than a whole mountain of books, photos and leaflets that cannot be incorporated and viewed satisfactorily.

NEVER write out the talk itself on overhead projector acetates or PowerPoint.

Use projections to show extra information or diagrams that assist the explanation. Think carefully about the placing of items. If possible make the speaker the centre of the presentation with a table containing the movable items at one side. A display of maps, pictures, posters and photographs could be on the other side, or if small, positioned on the table. Everything should be to hand so that the speaker does NOT have to be moving constantly from one side of the room to the other.

Always allow plenty of time for items to be viewed – NEVER 'flash' an article at the audience. Any circulation of items should be left until the end of the talk otherwise the audience will be viewing and not listening!

If electrical items are to be used – always set them up beforehand and check that they work. Nothing is more annoying for the audience than to be kept waiting whilst the speaker runs from one plug to another and plays with the television or video recorder!

Also, check that any slides or acetates are in the correct order and practise their display carefully before the actual presentation.

If using video – ensure that it is in the correct position and rehearse its integration into the presentation. Remember that it is a 'Talk' and not a 'Listen to the music' or 'Watch the television' session! Supporting aids should only make up a small section of any presentation so be very aware of how much time they will take up.

Visual aids can provide a speaker with a natural progression of thought and often enable the talk to be delivered without other memory aids such as cue cards.

Finally, write out the whole talk. Read it aloud and time it allowing extra time for the aids to be shown or used.

Points to remember:

- Be aware of your time scale

- Cut out any excess or choose additional material if it is required

- Practise with the script to ensure that the talk is the correct length

- Place key headings on to cue cards

NEVER use more than four cards and try if possible to keep headings down to one or two on each card.

NEVER write out the whole speech on to the cards because that will encourage READING rather than DIRECT TALKING!

'He who thinks by the inch and talks by the yard deserves to be kicked by the foot.'

Anon

The word **impromptu** means that what you do is prompted by the occasion rather than by advance planning. Consequently, when asked to give an impromptu talk or story, the candidate will either be given very little time to prepare - perhaps no more than half a minute or given subjects or titles to choose from 10 - 15 minutes before the examination commences. Obviously this kind of task, in the same way as sight-reading, depends very much upon **quickness of mind** and the ability to organize oneself very rapidly. In many Trinity examinations, an impromptu talk or story can be chosen by the candidate as an alternative to sight-reading.

Train students to make up their minds quickly when confronted with a **choice within a time limit**. Present students with a short list of possible impromptu talk titles and ask them to draw up a separate brainstorm spider for each title (see 10 PREPARED TALKS p.89). Each student will then be forced to decide which subject s/he thinks s/he knows most about and will be able to talk with greater **confidence**.

The brief **planning** should be similar to that recommended for prepared talks:

- Decide which three points will make up the gist of the talk

- Choose appropriate opening and closing statements

- Write brief cue cards

- Make NO attempt to compose the talk in full

- Rehearse in the mind the flow of the talk and linking of sections

- If there is a memory lapse when presenting look at the cue cards and think of the talk's progression

- Speak from knowledge

- Don't hesitate to express personal opinions and thoughts

When the talk is **completely impromptu** and there are only a very few moments . . . . . quickly decide:

Q How will you attempt to earn credit?

Q How will you project vivacity and enthusiasm?

Q How will you achieve fluency of communication?

Q Have you a good beginning and ending in mind?

Q How will you give shape to the talk?

Q Do you have the relevant information?

Q How can you show personal involvement?

How can a teacher help speakers?

Q How can a teacher foster appropriate techniques and develop speakers who 'think on their feet'?

USEFUL RESOURCE MATERIAL: **Graeme K Talboys'** *Aaargh to Zizz, 135 Drama Games* (see FURTHER READING) contains interesting and adaptable games for young people in the 10 – 18 year age range.

Here are some useful games that will build up sharpness, fluency and confidence.

BALL GAMES

1   In small circles or groups pass a soft ball around. Each person must say a word beginning with one letter of the alphabet, for example, B: Ball, Balloon, Boat, Beach, etc. If a word is repeated then the person who makes the repetition must sit down. Words should be spoken clearly and strongly so that everyone can hear.

2   One person stands in the centre of a group, thinks of an object and then states its initial letter, for example T, if s/he is thinking of Table. The ball passes around the circle until someone guesses the object. If the children are quite young the guessing can be limited to three times around the circle and then clues can be given in the form of a mime or description.

3   A similar game can be played requiring each person to say a word beginning with the following letter of the alphabet <u>either</u> randomly e.g. Apple, Bed, Cloud, Dream, etc. <u>or</u> related to a common theme e.g. Apple, Bread, Cake, Doughnut, Éclair, etc.

4   Again passing a ball, play 'word association' e.g. Fire, Engine, Water, Drink, Eat, etc. no word should be repeated and each must have a link with the one said immediately before.

5   Pass the ball delivering a word that has verbal dynamism or is onomatopoeic. Ask students to colour each word and give it life e.g. Glitter, Ripple, Shivering, Splash, etc. Words need not be connected.

6   These ball games can be developed into ones that involve creating stories. Stop any of the above games and ask students to use the last 2, 3 or 4 words as part of a story, e.g. Glitter, Ripple, Shivering, Splash could inspire a story about the sea. Encourage dramatic openings such as 'The waves lashed the shore and the wind howled as David struggled to bring the boat into the harbour.' Each person can give one sentence or leave the story on a 'cliff hanger', for example, 'the boat began to spin around and suddenly . . . . .'

7   In a variation of the previous game each person gives only one word - although this is quite difficult because no one can really control the story.

These games encourage alacrity and development of vocabulary, and it will be quite natural to move on from these kinds of activity to the giving of spontaneous talks.

SPONTANEOUS TALKS

In groups, **each member will talk for half a minute** on: 'My Family, My School, My Pet, My Best Friend' or a similar subject. One member of the group should keep a check on the time and point to the next person as soon as thirty seconds have elapsed. Encourage students to speak slowly and keep the sentences short and to the point; discourage them from saying "*um*" or "*and um*" when a thought pause occurs or use meaningless phrases such as "*you know*". Soon the talking length can be extended to one minute, then two. Eventually the speaker will be able to communicate for several minutes on subjects with which s/he is familiar e.g. My Favourite Holiday, How To Play Tennis, Going Hiking, etc.

A talk could develop into an explanation of something e.g. How to get to school from home, to the cinema or the swimming pool. Vary the manner of travel: walking, cycling, going on the bus or by car, etc.

Various examination boards have Communication Syllabuses, which contain a variety of ideas that can be used to develop 'show and tell' skills.

SHOW AND TELL GAMES

1   **Various objects could be introduced** such as a postcard, a horseshoe, a wrapped present, a broken toy, a Halloween mask, etc. and each student then asked to share a relevant memory associated with one of them.

2   **Tools and gadgets could be introduced** such as a tin opener; a screwdriver; a camera; a torch, etc. and students asked to explain how the items are normally used.

INTERVIEWS

Mock interviews can be held:

1   **Interview for employment.** One student (or several) chooses the job s/he would like to apply for and another acts as the interviewer.

2 **The interview is for radio or television** – and one of the students could pretend to be someone famous. (This requires a little research.)

3 **Interview for an unknown job.** A game that causes amusement is for a student to be interviewed for a job for which **only the interviewer has the job description**. One student is sent out of the room whilst the rest of the group is told the job title by the interviewer. When the student returns, the interviewer will endeavour to give clues by means of the questions s/he asks. The interviewee should try to determine what the job is!

If students have already undertaken several prepared talks they will be aware of how to **begin and end**. They should quickly choose an appropriate opening and then try to return to it at the end of the presentation. One device is to use questions for the opening. This can be effective when delivering an impromptu speech. No answers should be expected of course, but the use of **rhetorical questions** is certainly a good way to involve the listener.

Use personal experience and memories as much as possible. Include demonstrations if appropriate and quote from poems, plays or well-known proverbs. Reference can be made to television programmes, books or music. Make the whole talk lively and interesting. Try not to generalize but be specific, giving personal thoughts and opinions.

Practise different types of talks both explanatory and persuasive. **Explanatory** talks require basic information and often have need of demonstrations in addition. **Persuasive** talks require an enthusiastic voice and positive ideas to encourage the audience to undertake or be involved in the subject of the speech.

Realize that subjects can be dealt with in a variety of ways:

> ➤ **Travel** might concentrate on: (i) Methods of travel – planes, boats, trains, cars, horses, etc. (ii) A particular holiday that involved travelling (iii) How to prepare for travel - clothes, documents, injections, a budget, etc. (iv) a memorable flight (v) learning to horse ride, etc.

> ➤ **Keep fit** might concentrate on: (i) demonstrating exercises (ii) a particular sport (iii) diet (iv) team activities (iv) healthy eating (v) walking – the equipment required such as suitable clothing, shoes, maps, compass, etc.

> **Reading** might concentrate on: (i) a particular book (ii) a particular author you admire and would like to recommend (iii) a library (iv) the World Wide Web (v) literary fashions and fads, etc.

An awareness of **current affairs** and familiarity with **literature** will always aid the speaker.

Remember - the more **practice** undertaken, the easier it is to make an impromptu speech.

12 STORY TELLING

In most of Trinity's speech and drama examinations candidates are given the opportunity to spontaneously create and tell a story rather than read at sight. Students who want to try this option would benefit from the BALL GAMES (11 IMPROMPTU TALKS AND STORIES p.96) and when they build a degree of confidence they can experiment with different styles of story.

Here are some additional games that will assist students to tell spontaneous stories effectively:

STORY TELLING GAMES

1   Look at a picture and create a story about it. Consider what might have happened before the picture and what might happen afterwards.

2   Pick an object out of a bag and describe it to someone who is blindfolded.

3   Pick an object out of a bag and pretend it is not what it seems. It has magic properties. Convince the audience of its magical powers.

4   Pick an object out of a bag and imagine that the object has a strange tale to tell.

5   Place papers in a hat on which statements, instructions and questions are written such as: 'The old castle had an eerie atmosphere', 'Do it immediately' or 'What colour was it?' A story must be told that includes the sentence or sentences picked out of the hat.

6   Give three words that must be included in a story such as 'dragon', 'child', and 'journey'. Eventually increase this to four or five.

7   Show a picture or pictures that must set the scene or character/s that must be included in a story such as: a tropical beach scene on a postcard, cuttings from newspapers or magazines featuring famous people or places, book illustrations, etc.

Some final advice:

➢ When creating a story always ask yourself these questions: Shall I make it a dramatic story? A sad or emotional one? Do I use humour? The picture or given words will often lend themselves to one particular type of story.

➢ **Endeavour to create a strong opening**. Hold the given words in the mind and then use them as soon as possible.

➢ **Make the ending very definite** and if the opportunity arises give the ending an unusual twist.

➢ **Use personality and plenty of attack.** Communicate with firm crisp diction and share the story with lively facial expression.

Enriching practical work by understanding facts and principles

'One who asks a question is a fool for five minutes; one who does not ask a question remains a fool forever.'

Chinese proverb

During the course of the last 100 years significant advances have been made in our understanding of how voice, speech and communication work. As we established in the first chapter of this book, various theories about speech and drama were developed from the very earliest times. Then during the 20th century, huge amounts of research were done in the fields of **linguistics and semiotics.**

Linguistics is the study of human language – particularly spoken language:

- its structure

- how it is used to represent meaning

- how it is used to communicate ideas

- how it is formed

- how it is decoded

Semiotics, sometimes called **semiology**, is the study of signs and sign-using behaviour.

The subject of Speech and Drama is both an art and a science. The best practitioners always seek to know more, to understand more, never putting their heads in the sand and thereby ignoring highly relevant investigation and discovery. Bad practice in speech and drama usually stems from fossilized ideas – a refusal to rethink and explore.

Many examinations in Speech and Drama require candidates to demonstrate knowledge and understanding of vocal production and delivery – an awareness that should lead to better practical work. Furthermore it is also very important to think carefully about how drama works.

Theatre communicates through a series and pattern of signs. Whenever you are present during an act of theatre you respond in various ways to particular sights and sounds, and to the ways in which these relate to each other. Signs are sent to the audience by the actors, by the director, by the author of the play, by the designers of settings, costumes, lighting, and so on. In any production there is a massive amount of meaning communicated through signs. At the heart of the signing process is the **actor, his/her body, his/her movements and his/her** speech. All movements and sounds made by actors are signs, and the actor himself/herself is a sign. These considerations are usually now called the **semiotics of theatre,** a sub-discipline of semiotics.

One of the founders of semiotics, the Swiss linguist **Ferdinand de Saussure,** introduced a vitally important key concept when he made a clarifying distinction between the two fundamental components of communication:

> ➤ the **signifier** – the sign itself, the physical object/s or sound/s

> ➤ the **signified** – the concept or idea behind the sign

Poor speech and drama work results when there is a lack of fusion between these two essential components. To borrow one of **Shakespeare's** unbeatable descriptions, a lot of bad examination work is like:

> '. . . . . *a tale*
> *Told by an idiot, full of sound and fury,*
> *Signifying nothing.*'

USEFUL ADDITIONAL READING: *Thinking About Plays* by **Ken Pickering** and **Giles Auckland-Lewis.** This handbook encourages thinking about how drama works and suggests ways of looking at play texts and plays. (see FURTHER READING)

I *WHAT IS SPEECH?*

Speaking is made possible by a secondary use of a vital bodily process, that of respiration. Carbon dioxide needs to be constantly expelled from the lungs – most of the time silently but it is possible, by making various movements within the vocal tract, to modify, block and restrict the outgoing air stream, and create specific noises of different sorts. However, speech is obviously not just a string of sounds. It is organized in a hierarchical fashion:

- individual sounds are organized into syllables

- syllables are grouped to form words

- words are put together to form phrases

- phrases are put together to form sentences

- sentences are put together to form continuous speaking

CONSONANTS AND VOWELS

The smallest units of information when pronouncing a language are **consonants and vowels**. Standard pronunciation of English uses twenty distinctive vowel sounds and twenty-four distinctive consonant sounds. Linguists call these units **phonemes**. A phoneme is the smallest unit of sound that has the power to differentiate one word from another and thereby change meaning. For example, the words 'weak', and, 'peak' are differentiated by the **w** and **p** sounds at the start of each word. Phonemes combine in speech to form words that are recognized by someone who speaks the language containing the words. Phonemes are defined in terms of what the listener perceives, NOT in terms of the actual sounds themselves. e.g. most English speakers would actually speak 'in bed' as 'im bed' – an example of the highly common practice of **assimilation**, the process by which a segment of speech is modified by its 'next door neighbour' although the listener would almost certainly 'hear' the phoneme '**n**' – and would hear the word 'in' even though it has not been said!

STRESS

Accurate pronunciation at the word level also requires accurate use of **stress** – stressing the appropriate syllable of a word. Stressing a syllable is to utter the vowel in the syllable more prominently i.e. slightly longer, louder and/or higher than the other syllables. This contrast has a tremendous effect on how words sound and can even change a word's meaning. e.g. 'insight' and 'incite' are distinguished wholly by a difference in stressing – the two words have exactly the same vowel and consonant sounds (ignore the spelling!). Amusingly, when people from England visit certain countries, they are momentarily confused when offered '**des**ert' in restaurants: they hear the word as one that refers to a sandy wasteland – 'de**ssert**' and '**des**ert' are distinguished aurally chiefly by the fact that one is weak/strong, while the other is strong/weak; also, observe that '**per**vert (noun) is distinguished from 'per**vert**' (verb) almost entirely through stress contrast – just like other pairs of words such as 'in**cline**' (verb) and '**inc**line' (noun).

PHRASE

Linking the ends of words with the beginnings of the following words produces pronunciation that is beyond the word level – the level of a **phrase**. A phrase is usually a group of words (or sometimes a single word such as 'Yes' or 'No'), carrying a unit of meaning. e.g. 'When I' cannot be regarded as a phrase because it carries no meaning in its own right, whereas 'When I got up this morning' is an understandable unit of meaning. In effective speaking, phrases are spoken as 'chunks of meaning'.

PACE

Effective use of phrasing will involve a varied use of **pace,** which, in turn, affects the rhythm of the statements.

RHYTHM

Rhythm is an important consideration when speaking. Emphasising the important words of your statements and questions and reducing the less important words has a profound effect on how people understand you when you speak.

INTONATION

Another very important aspect of speaking at the phrase level is **intonation.** Producing the rising and falling tones of the language allows us to reveal our meaning more precisely and to speak more efficiently. We differentiate between certain questions and statements using intonation, we separate parts of statements with intonation, and our ability to produce short questions and responses accurately depends on our use of intonation. Effective speakers use intonation patterns to help them communicate their ideas. The rising and falling inflections separate ideas, distinguish questions and sentences, and show special emphasis. Spoken language gives us much more information than a string of words.

From the particular way a phrase is spoken we can deduce:

What is being emphasized or contrasted. e.g. 'She's wearing a RED dress' (everyone else is wearing blue . . . .)

Whether it is a question or a statement. e.g. 'You are coming to the party?

The attitude of the speaker to the statement. e.g. 'He won again' spoken happily/sadly.

II PHRASING

Some people get confused by the term 'phrase'. Examiners certainly sometimes hear a number of conflicting and inaccurate definitions offered by candidates.

Let's try to remove the mystique.

When we talk, we very rarely communicate by saying single words. We communicate rather through uttering units of meaning, usually made up of strings of words such as 'As I was on my way here', 'Once upon a time' or 'Are you all right? Sometimes a unit of meaning is complete in itself like the third example, 'Are you all right?' but more often than not a unit of meaning is not freestanding. It needs to link to one or more other phrases before the listener can comprehend a complete piece of sense. e.g. 'As I was on my way here' needs to connect to another phrase such as 'I met my brother'.

The definition of the word *phrase* is useful:

phrase   a brief expression, sometimes a single word, but usually two or more words forming an expression by themselves, or being a portion of a sentence

III *PAUSING*

We usually think of speech in terms of the separate words that it consists of when you transcribe the speaking into writing. However, the **actual** sound of speech is not split into words – there are usually no gaps at all between words in speaking. 'Once upon a time', for example would invariably be said as if it were a one five-syllable word:

wʌnsəponətaim – having a rhythm rather like 'unexpectedly' although the final syllable of this word would be less prominent than 'time'. A pause occurs whenever the syllables do not run together completely fluently: sound is halted briefly before it is resumed. Usually temporary suspension of sound takes place between phrases but occasionally pause can occur mid phrase, and when it does, this will always draw a special attention to the word or phrase immediately after the pause. e.g. 'She's . . . . . gone I'm afraid' or 'His name is . . . . . Lucifer'.

Poets sometimes deliberately suggest a special emphasis when they suspend the flow of a phrase from one verse line to the next – a phenomenon sometimes known as **enjambment**.

Take, for example, the first verse of **D H Lawrence's** poem *The Piano:*

> *Softly, in the dusk, a woman is singing to me;*
> *Taking me back down the vista of years, till I see*
> *A child sitting under the piano, in the boom of the*
> *tingling strings*
> *And pressing the small, poised feet of a mother who*
> *smiles as she sings.*

The poet's deliberate break of phrase occurs at the end of the second line. The other ends of lines coincide with ends of phrases.

NOTE: An absence of punctuation does not necessarily indicate that a phrase is not complete: 'in the boom of the tingling strings' is a complete phrase, even though it has no punctuation immediately after it.

The poet indicates a kind of pause after 'see', perhaps implying a slightly delayed memory, a recollection, which tends to give the image of the 'child sitting under the piano' a marked quality – to some extent because we had to wait slightly for it! A speaker can convey this slightly delayed fluency by using a slight pause at the end of line two, a pause that does not allow any suggestion of closure, a pause that is sometimes known as a **suspensive pause**.

IV *EMPHASIS*

Emphasis causes a particular word or group of words to stand out in a stream of speech. It is achieved through a range of means:

- variation of volume

- variation of length

- variation of pitch

- variation of pause

- variation of pace

- variation of gesture

- variation of facial expression

. . . . . and so on.

In III *PAUSING* (see p.118) we considered how a pause before a word provides that word with emphasis. NO change of pitch or volume needs to be employed when pause is used in this way.

Some aspects of delivery need to stand out in order to produce emphasis. Experiment with various means of emphasizing. Try bulging your eyes slightly on a particular word, stamping your foot or whispering. In most cases speakers emphasize through pitch inflection but APT variety is one of the essences of effective work in speech and drama.

V PACE

In Speech and Drama the word **pace** refers to the rate of speed at which an activity or movement proceeds. It is therefore possible both to talk about the overall pace of a dramatic scene and also about the pace of a particular part of the action within the scene. Generally the word pace is preferred to the word **speed** – because the word speed always implies 'speedy' to many people!

Pace, however, is a neutral term (like **colour**) and always needs further description. There are of course no fixed rules about rate/s of speed in speech and drama work. Appropriateness is the key, plus awareness that variety of pace is essential in any artistic work that uses the time dimension – the arts of music, dance, drama and speech.

When **speaking continuously**, appropriate variety of pace is essential. Some passages of language demand a faster delivery than others, and a dramatic extract usually needs to be spoken at a much faster rate than a piece of description. However, there are obvious outer limits. A pace that is too slow is difficult to listen to for very long because it gets boring! While a pace that is too rapid cannot accommodate clarity of articulation and the audience is left without specific understanding.

Always remember that effective speakers constantly vary three central musical dimensions:

- Volume

- Pitch

- Pace

VI *RELAXATION*

We have already established that speaking is made possible by secondary use of primary bodily processes. A controlled stream of air passing from the lungs through the larynx and causing the vocal cords to vibrate creates the sound that is produced during speech. To achieve free vibration of the vocal cords you need a relaxed throat. A tensed throat can cause your vocal cords to tighten which will make your voice sound strained. Furthermore, without a controlled flow of air, effective speech is NOT possible.

Good speech is dependent upon an adequate intake of breath followed by control of exhalation. Proper breathing for speech depends very much upon a relaxed body state. Therefore it is very important to be aware of any body tensions that might impede a fluent vocal process.

Relaxation exercises should be tried so that intrusive tensions are eliminated. Remember that when you are performing you are highly likely to produce extra tensions because of the nerves that are usually associated with the process. Performing or speaking in public is inclined to produce tension – even in the most experienced.

There is no set method of encouraging relaxation but any effective regime is likely to include some of the following exercises:

RELAXATION EXERCISES

1   Isolate the muscles in your body beginning with your toes. One by one contract each muscle area as tightly as you can, and then release completely. Focus on each of the parts of your body in turn, working upwards from your feet, and tense each group of muscles before relaxing them completely, so you feel the difference between tension and relaxation.

2   Upper-chest breathing not only tends to produce short shallow breaths but it also puts tension in the shoulders, neck and larynx, so it is important to learn to breathe deeply from the lower chest

(diaphragmatic breathing). Put your hands on your lower rib cage at the level of the diaphragm. Breathe in slowly and try to feel your lower-chest fill with air. Your hands should move apart from each other. Hold the breath for just a second, and then let it out slowly through a half open mouth on a quiet, gentle 'haaaah' sound. Do this several times.

3   Yawn or laugh. You can't do either if you are tense, so it will help to relieve tension. Check how your neck, shoulders and face are feeling. Do a few large movements to loosen face and throat muscles – pretend you are chewing food. With the palms of your hands, stroke slowly down the sides of your face just in front of your ears, encouraging your jaw to be free and relaxed. Let the jaw go completely slack. Nod your head up and down slowly, keeping your jaw slack – be aware of how your jaw closes slightly when you nod forward, and opens when you nod back. Try opening and closing your jaw by moving it with your hand just as you might move a puppet's jaw – trying not to let your jaw resist your hand.

4   Do one or two 'neck rolls' – drop your head to your chest and gently roll it first to one side and then the other, then to the front again. Bring your head upright

again in a very effortless way. Shrug your shoulders tightly up to your ears. Then let go of them completely. Finally try rubbing around your neck and throat to loosen any tightness.

 Useful tips:

- ➢ **Sip water** to combat dry mouth.
- ➢ **Avoid eating** immediately before any kind of performing.

VII *POSTURE*

Proper breath support is one of the most important factors in any form of speaking. Your voice IS air, and no vocalization is possible without it! So, the more efficiently you breathe, the more efficiently you will be able to sustain your voice and project it without strain. If you do not have a sufficient stream of breath to support your voice, you will find yourself running out of breath and your voice will sound thin when you speak.

For many people insufficient breath is caused by bad posture. We tend to slouch because of bad habits and effects of stress. Twenty first century life has created '21st century posture'. We use our bodies differently from how our ancestors did. We sit far more than a human body was designed to.

Poor posture automatically reduces the volume of the chest cavity, encouraging shallow breathing from the upper chest. If you breathe from the upper chest, only the upper lobes of the lungs are being used, and these have only a small volume of air - a small fraction of your full lung capacity. Furthermore, the upper rib cage is fairly rigid, so not much expansion of the ribs can take place up there.

In contrast, when you are in an upright yet relaxed state, the lower intercostals and diaphragm muscles are allowed free expansion and contraction, increasing the volume of air available for speech and enabling you to control the process and sustain the length and quality of your vocal delivery.

 To improve your posture you might find the following procedure helpful:

(i)   Stand with your feet apart with each foot more or less immediately below the shoulder above it. Lift your arms up to the ceiling and STRETCH. Hold for about 4 seconds and then allow your arms to flop freely and loosely by your sides.

(ii)   Now reach up to the ceiling with right arm only. STRETCH with that arm and then let it fall freely to your side. Shake it loosely. Do exactly the same with your left arm.

(iii)   Stand with your spine straight and your feet about shoulder-width part. Imagine that you are dangling from a puppet string fastened to the centre of the top of your skull. This body image should encourage you to feel tall, but with no sensation of rigidity. Gently shake out your arms and legs one by one – ensure that each is completely free. Lift your left shoulder high and tightly, and then let it loose and free – be aware of the difference in feeling. Repeat – concentrate on the contrast between tightness and looseness. Do exactly the same with your right shoulder – be aware of being tall at the centre of your body, keep your head level, eyes forward and feet facing in front of you.

(iv)   Let the head drop to the chest, allowing the neck muscles to relax completely. Now feel the head being drawn up by that puppet string. This procedure should ensure that you do not over-use your neck muscles. Your head should feel high, but not 'held' by your neck. Let the head drop again, let it rock from side to side, chin on your chest, and then allow the puppet string once again to draw your head to a tall, free position.

(v)   Slowly breathe in and out a few times, feeling that the lower part of your chest expands to some extent – but **out**wards, not **up**wards. Focus on the smoothness and quality of each breath.

(vi)   As you stand, remember that it is not your spine or neck that is keeping you upright – it is the puppet string at the top of your head that is suspending you.

(vii)   Next, imagine that the puppeteer suddenly lets go of the string at the top of your head. You will have no control over the top part of your body and it will flop down, your torso is hanging over your legs. As you flop over, let your breath come out of your body absolutely freely. Keep standing, but with your knees loose. Deliberately loosen and shake various parts of the upper body while in this position – shaking your head, shoulders, arms, and hands as if these parts belonged to a very floppy puppet!

(viii)   Imagine that the puppeteer now pulls you upright by means of the string attached to the top of your head. You will slowly uncurl, vertebra by vertebra into a free, upright position. As you uncurl, slowly breathe in.

(ix)   Repeat any of the above until you are confident that you have freed yourself from extraneous tension and have allowed the body the uprightness and freedom it needs for breathing and open vocalization.

Breathing for speech makes greater demands on the body than breathing for life. Speaking usually requires deeper, fuller breathing than is needed for biological purposes. For speech, inhalation needs to be made at particular intervals, and exhalation is more prolonged – after all, it is the exhalation that carries your utterance.

Effective speaking is a process of conveying your meaning in vocalized groups of thought. A speaker takes a different sized breath according to the length of what is to be said, the volume at which it is to be said, and the emotional state of the delivery. The rate of an effective speaker's breath can no longer be the normal pattern of fifteen to twenty breaths a minute with inhalation and exhalation taking approximately the same time. It will need to be sporadic and irregular, with quick inhalation and long, drawn out, controlled exhalations.

Breathing for biological purposes does not require any active effort to exhale – simply a relaxation of the muscles needed to inhale. **Effective speaking, however, cannot be maintained without controlled exhalation**. Air, especially oxygen, cannot be stored in the body in the same way that food and liquid can. Therefore, normal breathing is almost invariably an involuntary process. The diaphragm contracts, sometimes the chest cavity increases, and in order to maintain a certain level of pressure in the lungs, inhalation takes place. When the diaphragm relaxes, air is expelled from the lungs because the chest cavity becomes much smaller. By deliberately expanding the lower ribs when lowering the diaphragm, a greater volume of gas is automatically drawn into the lungs. By controlling the relaxation of the muscles between the ribs (the **intercostals**) and the diaphragm, you can be in command of the amount of air that is inhaled and expelled for vocal purposes.

It is important to work in harmony with your body's biological needs when doing breathing exercises. You must NEVER deny yourself breath – that will always, understandably, trigger tension. So a breathing method that satisfies both speech and biological needs is required, a method that allows air to move in and out of the lungs without much effort on the part of the speaker.

➤ In **clavicular breathing**, effort is centred in the upper chest, an area that has far less flexibility than the lower section of the chest where the diaphragm is situated and where the ribs are wider and more movable. Consequently, in order to inhale when using clavicular breathing, the entire rib cage has to lift, which involves the shoulders as well. This kind of breathing involves a lot of effort since a large portion of the skeleton is moving and the speaker is prevented from appearing to look at ease.

➤ On the other hand, when you employ **intercostal diaphragmatic breathing**, you use the lower part of the thorax – which is very well equipped to move, your diaphragm and your abdominal muscles. Breath support for your voice will then come from the abdominal muscles, NOT the upper chest or neck muscles.

Intercostal diaphragmatic breathing has proved to be a highly efficient method of breathing for speakers, actors and singers, and when it is properly applied it enables the performer to appear to be perfectly at ease.

To gain **abdominal support** for your voice, try the following exercises, keeping your shoulders, chest, and upper body still and relaxed.

BREATH EXERCISES

1   Inhale, encouraging the lower lungs fill deeply and allow the abdominal area (between your lower ribs and belly button) to relax and expand. Put your hand across the tummy between the bottom of the rib cage and your waist, the **epigastrium,** and feel it bulge slightly as you breathe in.

2   As you take a deep breath, encourage the bottom ribs to expand laterally. Imagine that there is a tyre inner tube around the lower ribs: (i) As the breath comes in, the tube inflates. (ii) As the breath goes out, the tyre deflates.

3   Be aware that your body can work like a 'bellows'. Lie on the floor with one hand loosely resting on the abdominal area (between your lower ribs and belly button). Take slow, steady breaths and feel your hand rise and fall: (i) Breathe in and your **epigastrium** rises. (ii) Breathe out and your **epigastrium** descends.

4   Breathe in to a count of 5, and then count to 5 as you exhale. Expand your breaths by breathing: in to 6, out to 6 . . . . . in to 7, out to 7 . . . . . in to 8, out to 8 . . . . . in to 9, out to 9 . . . . . in to 10, out to 10.

5   While on your back, breathe in deeply and then release the breath with a sigh. Turn the sigh into an 'Aw' sound. Feel that the breath is the 'centre' of the sound and that the sound is fully supported by the breath.

6   Try speaking words such as: WHY, HOW, STOP and GO with the same kind of breath support. Then support phases such as: I'M GOING, STAY HERE and LOOK AT THAT.

In biology, the word **organ** is a term given to any specific part of an organism that performs a **specific function** – such as an eye, wing, or leaf. We have already established that there are not really any organs of voice and speech, as such. All the organs used to produce utterance originally evolved for other purposes: such as the lungs for breathing, the vocal cords for preventing choking, the tongue for eating and tasting, the nose for breathing and smelling and the lips for eating. Fortunately, human beings have adapted these organs for crucial secondary purposes - the production of communicative noises!

These are the 13 principal parts of the body used for speaking listed in their order of use during speech:

> **Breathing apparatus**. This mechanism has been already been outlined in VIII *BREATHING FOR VOICE PRODUCTION* (see p.130).

> **Larynx**. This is the structure that holds and manipulates the **vocal cords**. You can feel its outline by touching the centre of your neck just below your chin. The larynx in men is usually more prominent – hence the term 'Adam's apple'! The opening between the vocal cords is called the **glottis.** The vocal cords are more like curtains

than 'cords'. They are folds of tissue stretched across the airway to the lungs and can vibrate against each other - providing much of the sound during speech.

➢ **Pharynx**. This is the cavity between the root of the tongue and the walls of the upper throat - a space that is an important vocal resonator.

➢ **Epiglottis**. This is the fold of tissue below the root of the tongue which helps cover the larynx during swallowing to ensure that food goes into the stomach and not the lungs! A few languages use the epiglottis in making sounds but English is not one of them. So you can ignore this organ as far as speech and drama in the English language is concerned!

➢ **Tongue**. This large organ moves to make vowels and many consonants.

➢ **Soft palate** or **velum**. This is the soft portion of the roof of the mouth positioned behind the hard palate. The tongue touches the velum when the three **velar** sounds of English are made, and the velum itself can move. If it lowers, it creates an opening that allows air to flow out through the nose; if it stays raised, the pathway to the nose is blocked.

➤ **Uvula**. This is the small, floppy organ at the back of the soft palate that vibrates for the **r** consonant in many French dialects – although this sound would normally be considered to be defective if used for the **r** consonant of English.

➤ **Nose**. The nasal cavities are used fully during the three **nasal** consonants. The nose also acts as an important organ of general resonance during all vocalization.

➤ **Hard palate**. This is the front, stiff portion of the roof of the mouth. The term **palate** by itself usually refers to the hard palate.

➤ **Mouth**. This very flexible cavity provides the specific resonances for all vowel sounds. It also acts as an important organ of general resonance during all vocalization.

➤ **Alveolar ridge**. This is the ridge just behind the upper teeth where there is a change in the angle of the hard palate. Sounds that are made while the tongue is in contact with the area between the upper teeth and this ridge are called **alveolars**.

➢ **Upper Teeth**. For **dental** sounds the upper teeth are used: they make contact with either the tongue or the lower lip.

➢ **Lips**. These are involved in the formation of **labial** sounds, either **bi-labial** (upper and lower lips) or **labio-dental** (lower lip and upper teeth).

X CONSONANTS

Consonants and vowels are produced by an interference of the flow of air through the mouth and sometimes the nose. Consonants are created when the airflow is obstructed and/or restricted at one of various locations along the vocal tract i.e. the place of articulation.

It is customary to give each consonant a 3-part label according to:

1   The **place** of articulation

2   What kind of **interference** of the air-stream is involved

3   The part played by the **vocal folds**. Whether or
         not they are vibrating while the consonant is
         formed (see **Voiced or voiceless?**).

As an example, the briefest specific description of a **b**
sound would be: **voiced bi-labial plosive**.

Voiced or voiceless?

If the vocal folds remain apart, the exhaled air can escape
unimpeded. Sounds produced in this way are described as
voiceless.

To sense the distinction between voiced and voiceless
sounds, place your fingers lightly on your Adam's apple.
Say a long **sssssss**. Then say a long **zzzzzzz**. Repeat
this contrast a few times. Similarly, try **fffffff** contrasted
with **vvvvvvv**. You should be able to detect some
vibration when you say **zzzzzzz** and **vvvvvvv** but no
vibration when you say **sssssss** and **fffffff**.

The voiced/voiceless distinction is important in the English
language because word meaning often depends on
whether that sound is voiced or not. For example, the
words 'big' and 'pig' are distinguished aurally purely by
whether or not the vocal cords are vibrating during the first
consonant – in all other respects the two words are exactly
the same!

Here is a chart containing a full list of the 24 English consonants, grouped in columns according to whether or not they are voiced.

NOTE: 8 voiceless consonants can be directly paired with 8 voiced ones i.e. they are identical in all other respects.

THE 24 ENGLISH CONSONANTS

VOICELESS	VOICED
p as in pear	b as in bear
t as in ten	d as in den
f as in fine	v as in vine
k as in cot	g as in got
s as in seal	z as in zeal
θ as in thigh	ð as in thy
ʃ as in masher	ʒ as in measure
tʃ as in cheer	dʒ as in jeer
h as in hire	
	r as in rear
	l as in leer
	m as in mere
	n as in near
	j as in year
NB: some speakers use a voiceless w when saying words spelled with 'wh' (like 'when')	w as in we're
	n as in ring

Manner of articulation

Once the breath has left the larynx, it passes into the vocal tract as: (i) vocalized air – **voiced** or (ii) unvocalized air – **voiceless**. Obstructing the airflow in different ways within the vocal tract then produces specific consonants. There are a number of locations at which these restrictions can take place known as the **places of articulation** and there are 6 principal types of obstruction that are commonly referred to as the **manner of articulation**.

PRINCIPAL TYPES OF OBSTRUCTION

1 **Plosive** consonants are sounds made by completely blocking the exhaled air. When the closure occurs, the air builds up behind the stoppage until the closure is released – making an explosion of breath, a sharp noise.

   If you say the sound **p**, you should be able to feel:

   • the build up of air before the sound is made

   • the **p** sound itself when your lips are released

   Plosive sounds CANNOT be prolonged. The releasing of the air causes an abrupt momentary sound, and once the air has been released, the sound has escaped.

The 6 plosive phonemes of English are: **p** (as in pear), **b** (as in bear), **t** (as in ten), **d** (as in den), **k** (as in cot) and **g** (as in got).

2 **Fricative** consonants are sounds made by forcing air through a narrow gap so that a vibrating noise is created. If you say a prolonged **ffffff** sound, you should be able to feel the friction occurring between the upper teeth and the lower lip.

You will find that you can maintain a fricative sound for as long as your breath lasts – in absolute contrast to plosive sounds.

The 7 fricative phonemes of English are: **s** (as in seal), **z** (as in zeal), **θ** (as in thigh), **ð** (as in thy), **ʃ** (as in masher), **ʒ** (as in measure) and **h** (as in hire).

3 **Nasal** consonants are sounds made by air escaping through the nose rather than the mouth. The oral cavity is blocked at one of three locations to stop air escaping through the mouth, while the soft palate is lowered to allow air to pass through the nose.

If you say a prolonged **m** sound and put your hand in front of your mouth you will actually feel the vocalized air is escaping through the nose.

The 3 nasals of English are: **m** (as in <u>m</u>ere), **n** (as in <u>n</u>ear) and **ŋ** (as in ri<u>ng</u>).

NOTE: All nasal consonants are voiced.

4   **Lateral** consonants are sounds made by the tongue causing an obstruction at a point along the centre of the mouth but the sides of the tongue are left low so that breath can escape over its sides.

l (as in <u>l</u>eer) is the only **lateral phoneme** in English.

NOTE: Both the clear and dark versions of the phoneme are lateral sounds.

5   **Affricate** consonants are sounds made when plosives are immediately followed by fricatives at the same place of articulation. Since affricates are made up of two combined sounds, phonetic representations of them always feature two symbols – the plosive followed by the fricative.

The 2 affricate phonemes of English are: **tʃ** (as in <u>ch</u>eer) and **dʒ** (as in <u>j</u>eer).

6   **Approximant** consonants are sounds that have a quality somewhat similar to that of vowels, despite

the fact that they undoubtedly function as consonants in the language i.e. they precede or follow the vowel sounds, which occur at syllable peaks – the most sonorous parts of any utterance.

Approximants are briefer, less stable and have closer articulation than vowels but their similarity in sound to vowels has led to their sometimes being called **semivowels**. In articulating approximants, the speech organs produce a narrowing of the vocal tract but leave enough space for air to flow without audible friction. Because of this, **frictionless continuant** is yet another term that has sometimes been used for this category of consonant. What's more, when approximant consonants precede vowels, they are sometimes called **glides**!

The 3 approximant phonemes of English are: **r** (as in rear), **j** (as in year) and **w** (as in we're).

Places of articulation

Glottal sounds are those made in the larynx through the closure or narrowing of the glottis. The sound **h** (as in hire) is the only glottal phoneme in the English language – a **glottal fricative**. The **glottal stop** or **glottal plosive** is a sound that is used very commonly but it is not a phoneme since it CANNOT change word meaning. It is often used as an alternative sound for **t**, between vowels and at ends of words.

NOTE: The glottal stop is never substituted for a **t** at the beginning of words.

When listeners hear a glottal stop they 'translate' it into the **t** phoneme. e.g. wɔʔə is heard as wɔtə (water). You also use your glottis for continuous speech sometimes, when you **whisper.**

Velar sounds are made when the back of the tongue is pressed against the soft palate. The soft palate can be felt with your tongue if you curl it as far back and as high as you can. Velar phonemes are the **voiceless plosive k** (as in c̲ot), the **voiced plosive g** (as in g̲ot) and the **voiced nasal ŋ** (as in riŋg̲).

Palatal sounds are formed at the arched bony structure that constitutes the roof of the mouth. The clearest example of a palatal sound within the English phoneme system is **j** (as in y̲ear). You might feel a little friction when the sound is forced between the tongue and the palate but it is not an obvious fricative sound. There is not much in the way of restriction (compare its sound to a definite fricative such as **v**), so it has traditionally often been known as a **semivowel** i.e. its quality is close to the unrestricted quality of a vowel sound.

There are 4 other sounds known as **palato-alveolar**. These are made when the blade of the tongue straddles both the alveolar ridge and the front of the hard palate as air is forced through.

These phonemes are: ʃ (as in ma<u>sh</u>er), **ʒ** (as in mea<u>s</u>ure), tʃ (as in <u>ch</u>eer) and dʒ (as in <u>j</u>eer).

Alveolar sounds are made when the tongue tip or **blade** touches the bony prominence behind the top teeth. 2 alveolar sounds are plosives, 2 are fricatives, 1 is a nasal and 1 is a lateral.

These are: **t** (as in <u>t</u>en), **d** (as in <u>d</u>en), **s** (as in <u>s</u>eal), **z** (as in <u>z</u>eal), **n** (as in <u>n</u>ear) and **l** (as in <u>l</u>eer).

Dental sounds are made when the teeth are involved in creating a fricative. Air is <u>either</u> forced between the upper teeth and the tongue: **θ** (as in <u>th</u>igh) and **ð** (as in <u>th</u>y) <u>or</u> between the upper teeth and the bottom lip: **f** (as in <u>f</u>ine) and **v** (as in <u>v</u>ine). Dental consonants that are made with upper teeth and the bottom lip are often called **labio-dentals**.

Bi-Labial sounds are made when the two lips are used to create the air obstruction.

In English there are 2 plosive bi-labials: **p** (as in pear), **b** (as in bear) and 1 nasal: **m** (as in mere).

Here is a full consonant chart containing all of the 24 English consonants, grouped in columns and rows according to manner and place of articulation. Voiced consonants are underlined.

NOTE: Each phonetic symbol used has been given a corresponding English word sound in the chart on p.139.

CONSONANT CHART

	bilabial	labio-dental	dental	alveolar	palato-alveolar	palatal retroflex	palatal	velar	glottal
plosive	p<u>b</u>			t<u>d</u>				k<u>g</u>	
fricative		f<u>v</u>	θ<u>ð</u>	s<u>z</u>	ʃ<u>ʒ</u>				h
nasal	<u>m</u>			<u>n</u>				<u>ŋ</u>	
lateral				<u>l</u>					
affricate					tʃ <u>dʒ</u>				
approximant	<u>w</u>					<u>r</u>	<u>j</u>		

Vowels differ from consonants in that the vocal tract is unobstructed during their formation. Air escapes in a comparatively free way through the mouth, and although the tongue, jaw and lips shape the vocal tract in different ways to create various vowel sounds, airflow is NEVER impeded while vowels are being uttered.

There are 3 major types of vowel:

- **single** position vowels – **monophthongs**

- **double** position vowels – **diphthongs**

- **triple** position vowels – **triphthongs**

There is a tremendous diversity of accents of the spoken English language, and almost all of this diversity is heard because of variant positions of the mouth assumed for vowel sounds. For example, when a Canadian says the word 'ask', it is likely to be said with an intermediate tongue height (æsk). Someone from the southeast of England, however, invariably says the same word with a low tongue height (ɑsk). It is therefore impossible to precisely categorize vowels as we have done with the consonants. To do that each of the innumerable accents of the English language would need its own separate chart!

Received Pronunciation (**RP**) is a very well known accent of British English – used extensively in the theatre, in broadcasting and in teaching English to foreign learners. So we shall base our analysis of vowel sounds on this particular accent. In doing so we are not implying that this accent is superior to others. It is an accent in the exactly the same way that any other pronunciation system is – but its familiarity is useful to us when we are discussing vowel sounds.

A **monophthong** is a vowel articulated without any noticeable change in quality throughout the course of a syllable, as in the vowel of the word 'let'.

The word monophthong comes from the Greek: *monophthongos, mono = single* and *phthongos = sound.*

The following chart shows the monophthongs of standard British English arranged with notional tongue height represented vertically and tongue forwards-backwards displacement represented horizontally. The chart is based on the position of the tongue's highest part in the mouth when uttering each vowel – imagining that we could see it from the left side of the face through the cheek!

MONOPHTHONGS OF STANDARD BRITISH ENGLISH

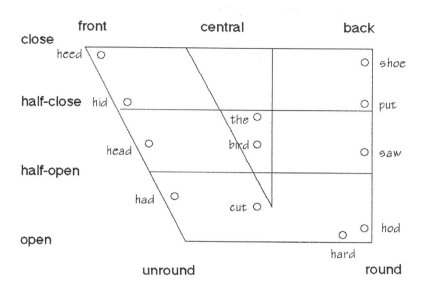

A **diphthong** is a vowel that is created by a glide from one vowel position to another within the same syllable, as in the vowel of the word 'lie'. The first part of a diphthong is always longer and stronger than the second part: then as the diphthong moves into the second vowel sound, the loudness decreases.

The word comes from the Greek: *diphthongos, di = two* and *phthongos = sound.*

NOTE: Entirely logically, phonetic representations for diphthongs always comprise of 2 syllables.

149

For English diphthongs in RP the **movement of the tongue** has 3 possible directions:

- **Higher towards the front** of the roof of the mouth i.e. in the general direction towards ɪ or **i**

- **Higher towards the back** i.e. in the general direction towards the ʊ or **u**

- **Towards a central area** i.e. in the general direction towards the ə

These 3 directions are usually known as **front closing**, **back closing** and **centring**.

1   There are 3 **front closing** diphthongs in RP. These can be heard in the words 'bay', 'by' and 'boy'.

2   There are just 2 **back closing** diphthongs in RP. These can be heard in the words 'no' and 'now'.

3   There are 3 **centring** diphthongs in RP. These can be heard in the words 'mere', 'mare' and 'moor'.

Triphthongs always consist of a movement or glide from one vowel to another and then onto a third.

The word comes from the Greek *triphthongos, tri = three* and *phthongos = sound.*

In English, triphthongs are always diphthongs followed by an extra schwa (neutral vowel) and the phonetic transcription for them always represents the ə.

The 5 kinds of English triphthong can be found in the following words:

player	=	pleɪə
fire	=	faɪə
royal	=	rɔɪəl
sour	=	saʊə
blower	=	bləʊə

The neutral vowel is the most common vowel sound in spoken English despite the fact that it occurs only in unstressed syllables. The sound is made when the mouth, lips and tongue are completely relaxed (in neutral!). Described linguistically as a **'mid-central unrounded monophthong'** and commonly represented by the schwa symbol: ə.

The vowel does not have any normal spelling in written English — it is actually a 'collapsed' pronunciation of all kinds of syllables that would sound quite different if they were stressed. Notice carefully how all unstressed syllables in the following words take the neutral vowel — regardless of their English spellings:

nation	=	ˈneɪʃən
sister	=	ˈsɪstə
commence	=	kəˈmens
account	=	əˈkaʊnt
London	=	ˈlʌndən
precious	=	ˈpreʃəs
colour	=	ˈkʌlə
benevolance	=	bəˈnevələns
sustain	=	səˈsteɪn

It is also important to realize that some one-syllable words, many of them prepositions, should almost always be pronounced with a neutral vowel. A preposition describes a relationship between other words in a sentence. Therefore, a preposition such as 'of' or 'as' is rather meaningless and should not be stressed. Preposition words that 'collapse' to the neutral vowel are: of, as, at, to, an, and, from, than, that – əv, əz, ət, tə, ən, ənd, ðən, ðət. Certain words are spoken with a neutral vowel when they occur in particular unstressed positions: e.g. have, them, some, am, can, had, has, and shall.

NOTE: the words 'a' and 'an' are virtually always pronounced with a neutral vowel ə and ən, together with the word 'the' when it precedes a consonant e.g. the tour = ðə tʊə.

When you are speaking it is very important to use the neutral vowel liberally. DON'T be tempted to substitute full vowel sounds, as this would destroy the essential rhythms of continuous speech and cause your speech to become unnatural and unclear. All good dictionaries indicate the syllables of multi-syllabic words that should be spoken with the neutral vowel.

XII RESONANCE

Resonance is the quality imparted to voiced speech sounds by the action of the resonating chambers of the throat, mouth and nasal cavities. The cavities of your head and neck act as resonators and determine the **tone** or **quality** of your voice when vocal vibrations pass through your vocal tract – which includes the pharynx, or throat, and mouth resonators. According to the size and shape of the throat and head cavities, certain aspects of the sound made by the vocal folds will be amplified and others will be suppressed. This phenomenon is known as resonance.

You should aim to have a full and balanced use of all your natural resonators. Think for a moment about the best and most expensive kind of stringed instrument. What chiefly determines its quality?

Why, its wooden resonating body, of course. Now think about the difference between the sound of a piano before and after its wooden body or **resonator** has been removed. You have surely heard the honky-tonk sound of a piano without its resonator! It is the fine, full resonating chamber that is responsible for the richer and superior tone of a grand piano.

Obviously, the human speaker or singer cannot purchase an instrument as a means to better resonance but fortunately the potential for fuller and richer resonance is built into your body. You are both the instrumentalist and the instrument itself.

To develop an open resonant voice you should:

> ➤ Make sure you keep a good alignment of your head, neck and spine so that all resonating channels are open and check that your jaw is not clenched – there should be some space between the upper and lower teeth.

> ➤ Make sure that you rely on the lower rib cage and diaphragm for vocal power. NEVER try to use the throat for power – you will only squash your pharynx resonance and tire or even cause strain and pain to your voice. It is impossible to get vocal power from the throat. Whenever you are speaking or singing, make sure you maintain a constant support of breath from below.

> ➤ Endeavour to fill all throat mouth and head cavities with open sound as the voice passes out of the body.

> ➤ Whenever you are speaking or singing, endeavour to release a channel of unrestricted sound through the mask of your face and forwards towards the listener.

Resonance has another important part to play in speech. All **vowel sounds** are in fact different kinds of specific resonance. You know already that you can alter the size and shape of your mouth cavity by moving your lips, tongue, lower jaw and soft palate. Such actions create different and particular sized and shaped resonating spaces in your mouth and these are responsible for the different vowel colours.

Q Have you ever wondered why the sound ooooooo is so different from the sound eeeeeee?

It's because their harmonic structures are so different, and these harmonic structures are created by the different positions of the mouth. Say, or sing on one pitch, a long ooooooo vowel sound and change it to eeeeeee, back to ooooooo, back to eeeeeee, etc, and you will hear and feel the repeatedly altered resonance.

XIII *INFLECTION*

Inflection or **inflexion** refers to a significant **alteration of vocal pitch** or **fundamental frequency**. It is helpful when considering the use of pitch in speech to think in terms of rising and falling inflections – in contrast to monotone or chanting which keeps a constant, level pitch. Any change or modification in the pitch of the voice can be called inflection.

Pitch is used in a great variety of ways in world languages. It is important to distinguish **tones** from **intonation**. In Linguistics, tones are pitches or inflections that signal word meaning. English is not a tone language and does not use tones in this manner. Intonation, on the other hand, refers to the control of pitch over large units, like phrases.

When your respiratory system prepares itself to provide the breath for voice, your vocal folds begin to approximate each other. Once they are closed sufficiently, the outgoing air sets them into **vibration**. Your brain provides continually changing impulses to the muscles operating the vocal folds to control the adjustments that create pitch inflections. This is done purely 'by ear': you CANNOT control the vibration of your vocal folds physically – it is not possible.

Awareness and regulation of vocal pitch must be done solely through building up greater aural awareness. When you vocalize, you 'think' pitch before physically producing it. That's all you can do. For any other musical instrument you would have to carefully and correctly manipulate the physical means such as the piano keys or pipe stops to produce correct pitch. For voice you turn the thought into sound! Quite remarkable, isn't it?

Varied use of inflection plays a major role in good vocal **modulation** – the variation of the musical features of speaking such as speed, pause, rhythm, pitch, tonal quality and volume.

NOTE: Ear training is an invaluable way of stimulating a greater musical awareness of pitch changes in speaking.

There are 5 basic types of inflection you should try to identify aurally and reproduced vocally:

- simple rising ↗

- simple falling ↘

- fall/rise ∪

- rise/fall ∩

- level pitch (absence of inflection!) →

Try each inflection on a simple word like 'yes' or 'well'.

Next, think about which part of a speaker's **pitch range** is being employed for an inflection i.e. the difference between a **high fall** and a **low fall** or between a **high rise** and a **low rise**. This kind of ear training is similar to that used in music but remember that for speaking we invariably use **gliding pitch** rather than **sustained pitch**.

XIV *INTONATION*

Most people with little or no experience in Speech and Drama become aware that what we want to convey to one another depends as much on HOW we say something as on WHAT it is that we actually say. It is obviously possible to use the same string of words to convey a huge variety of meanings, intentions, attitudes and moods.

One of the most important tools for doing this is our use of **intonation** – the vocalizing of distinctive vocal melodies that enables us to communicate so much more than the words, phrases and sentences alone. Although intonation is created chiefly by variations in pitch, **stress** and **rhythm** are also involved in creating spoken melodies.

In addition to conveying a huge range of expressive meaning e.g. enthusiasm, astonishment, fear, delight, exasperation, incredulity, etc. intonation also serves a **grammatical** function – differentiating between one type of sentence or phrase and another.

Thus, 'You live here', concluding with a low falling inflection, is heard by the listener as a simple assertion; whereas 'You live here?' said with a rising inflection on the final word is heard by the listener as a question.

XV VERSE FORM

All acts of communication are made up of two essential parts – just like coins. A coin comprises of two sides, often referred to as 'heads' and 'tails'. The two are distinctive but inseparable – each belongs, with equal importance, to the same entity. When you truly communicate, your act of communication invariably has **content** and **form**:

- WHAT you want to say

- the WAY it is said

This principal holds, no matter what kind of communication we consider:

- public speaking

- acting

- the visual arts

- instrumentalists

- novelists

. . . . . and so on.

In **verse**, the form may be understood to be its **structure** – the design of the poem's contents to convey intricate meanings and effects. Verse form may include the shape of the poem on the page, choice and construction of language, and 'sound' devices such as metre, rhyme and alliteration. A poem's form is best thought of as the way it combines all these various elements into a pattern within which each ingredient contributes to the work's purpose, impact and meaning.

Rhyme occurs when there is a correspondence of sound in the terminating words or syllables of two or more lines, one succeeding another immediately or at no great distance. Words or syllables used in this way must not begin with the same consonant, and if one begins with a vowel the other must begin with a consonant. The vowel sounds and accents must be the same, as well as the sounds of the final consonants if there are any.

Stress is a word that is used in a number of ways and is widely assumed to have a number of definitions. However, in the field of language it is a technical term used to refer to the degree of force used in producing a syllable. The usual distinction is between **stressed** and **unstressed** syllables – with the former being more prominent than the latter. The prominence is usually due to an increase in volume of the stressed syllable but increases in length and pitch may also contribute to the overall impression of prominence. In phonetic transcription a single inverted comma is used immediately before all stressed syllables:

ˈdɪfɪkəlt	difficult
ˈfəʊtəʊ	photo
bɪˈtwiːn	between
əˈnʌðə	another
ˈsʌmθɪŋ	something
kənˈtrəʊlə	controller
ˈkærɪktə	character
pəˈzɪʃən	position
ˈlæŋgwɪdʒɪz	languages
hɪmˈself	himself

Note that this simple but effective stress-marking method can be used without phonetically transcribing the symbols:

'difficult; 'photo; be'tween; a'nother; 'something; con'troller; 'character; pos'ition; 'languages; him'self.

Metre in verse is normally based on the more or less regular alternation of a particular pattern of stressed and unstressed syllables – and the basic repeated pattern is usually called a **foot**. The pattern of a foot can take one of five forms and it is the repetition of the particular pattern of stressed and unstressed syllables which gives us a sense of the 'beat' of a poem – its metre.

Let's look at examples of each of the 5 kinds of foot.

1   An **iamb** (di 'dum) is pronounced 'I am'. This particular pattern of foot is extremely common in English poetry. In the following couplet by **Carl Sandberg**, we hear twelve regular feet, each comprising of an unstressed syllable followed by a stressed one.

I 'wish to 'God I 'never 'saw you, 'Mag.
I 'wish you' never 'quit your 'job and 'came a'long with 'me.

1   The **trochee** ('dum di) is less common but was made very famous by the 19th century poet **Henry Wadsworth Longfellow**. In the following couplet we hear eight regular feet, each comprising a stressed syllable followed by an unstressed one.

'*There he* 'sang of '*Hia*'watha,
'*Sang the* 'Song of '*Hia*'watha.

2   The *spondee* ('dum 'dum – as in 'home-made') is quite rare. Normally when two syllables or two words are side by side, one of them will invite more weight than the other, so there can never be an unvarying use of the spondee foot – not even as much as a full line. However, when **William Shakespeare's** Hamlet says the following line we hear it begin with three spondees – three regular feet, each comprising a stressed syllable followed by another stressed one.

'*Thoughts*' black '*hands* 'apt, '*drugs* 'fit, and '*time a*'greeing.

3   The *anapaest* (di di 'dum) is a metrical foot consisting of three syllables, the first two being unstressed and the last stressed. In the following line by **Lewis Carrol**, we hear four regular anapaest feet.

To the 'horror of '*all who were* 'present that '*day*.

4   The *dactyl* ('dum di di) is metrical foot consisting of three syllables, the first being stressed and the last two unstressed. In the following couplet by **Alfred, Lord Tennyson** we hear four regular dactyl feet.

> " 'Forward, the 'Light Brigade!
> 'Charge for the 'guns!" he said.

These technical terms, which come to us from classical metrics, are used merely as convenient labels. The terms themselves don't need to be learnt by heart. However, when you are preparing your speaking of English poetry, it is very important to be aware of the potential effect of metre – it is a **vital** ingredient in poetry, deliberately and consciously used by most poets. You have to recognize metre and decide how much of it you will highlight when you speak the poem. This of course will depend upon the style of the verse. Much of **Banjo Patterson's** verse, for example, HAS to be delivered with some acknowledgement of the part played by the metre:

> The mountain road goes up and down
> From Gundagai to Tumut Town
> And, branching off, there runs a track
> Across the foothills grim and black,
> Across the plains and ranges grey
> To Sydney city far away.

On the other hand, if you were to deliver '*If music be the food of love play on*' emphasizing that it is a five foot line of regular iambs '*If **mu**sic **be** the **food** of **love** play **on***' – you would almost certainly destroy the delicate nature of the poetry.

This famous opening line of *Twelfth Night* is a rare example of an absolutely regular **iambic pentameter.**

pentameter a verse line of five metrical feet

The metre is one of the best known and most widely used metrical patterns in English poetry . . . . but why?

Iambic pentameter is so close to the natural rhythms of English speech that it is easy to adapt to different levels of language. Good iambic pentameter does NOT sound like a series of identically measured lines, it sounds like a series of subtle variations on a theme.

NOTE: In fact **Shakespeare** did not often write regular lines such as the one we've just considered.

Blank verse is simply iambic pentameter that is **unrhymed.** Whereas rhymed verse tends to be written in **stanzas.**

stanzas   *groups of lines arranged together, usually of regular lengths of between four and twelve lines, defined by their rhyme scheme and metrical pattern*

Poems written in blank verse tend to be divided into 'verse paragraphs' of varying lengths.

The natural speech rhythm of the English language is iambic, and the typical length of an utterance is often about ten syllables – the length most people can speak comfortably without pausing to take a breath. Therefore English speech rhythms fall quite naturally into iambic pentameter, and this harmony with the natural rhythms of ordinary speech accounts for the widespread use of blank verse in drama, dramatic monologues, epic poems, narrative poems, and long introspective or meditative poems.

Q   But why should a poet choose to write in blank verse if it often sounds so much like everyday speech?

Well, that's a very important question to ask when preparing to speak blank verse. **Shakespeare** often wrote in prose. In fact one of the most 'poetic' pieces of language in existence is surely Hamlet musing on the skull:

Alas, poor Yorick! I knew him, Horatio: a fellow of infinite jest, of most excellent fancy: he hath borne me on his back a thousand times.

It's in prose!

Poetry is often found in prose form – look at the play *Under Milk Wood* by **Dylan Thomas**. Verse always contains features not present in prose, and blank verse is NEVER merely prose. Although natural English speaking is often roughly of an iambic pentameter pattern, it constantly departs from that pattern, and frequently interrupts it with pauses and other unpredictable features. The rhythm of blank verse is more formal and more regular than the looser rhythmic pattern of normal speech.

Rhythm has to do with any regular recurrence of movement or variation. It has a relationship to metre but has a looser, wider application e.g. *'the rhythm of the tides'*.

NOTE: Metre comes from a Latin word and rhythm comes from the Greek

metron   *a strict measure of length*

rhuthmo   *to flow*

NOTE: That some of these categories and terms have already been given fuller consideration in 3 POETRY SPEAKING (see p.9).

Useful definitions when considering and discussing poetry:

ALLITERATION *repetition of an initial consonant e.g. Peter Piper picked a peck of pickled peppers.*

ASSONANCE *correspondence of accented vowels but not of the consonants e.g. 'main', 'came'*

BALLAD *a narrative poem, sometimes of folk origin and intended to be sung, consisting of simple stanzas and usually having a refrain*

BURLESQUE *satirical imitation or representation of a serious literary work or genre, usually applying the imitated form to inappropriate subject matter*

CAESURA *a break or pause in a line of verse dictated by sense or natural speech rhythm rather than by metrics*

DRAMATIC MONOLOGUE *a poem (usually lyrical) in which a speaker unintentionally reveals his or her character, often in relation to a critical situation or event, in a monologue addressed to the reader or to a presumed listener*

ELEGY *the term was usually used in classical times for love poetry written with a specific metre, since the 17th century it has come to mean a formal poem of lament and consolation concerning a particular person's death, or reflection on death in general*

EPIC *an extended narrative poem celebrating the exploits and achievements of heroes and/or divine characters in stately formal verse*

EPIGRAM *a very short, pithy poem expressing a single witty thought or observation*

FREE VERSE *verse deliberately employing irregular rhythmical patterns and absence or irregularity of rhyme*

IDYL *(i) either a short poem depicting simple scenes of pastoral, domestic, or country life, usually in idealized term (ii) or a more descriptive or narrative poem treating an epic or romantic theme*

INTERNAL RHYME the rhyming of a word or group of syllables in a line or verse, as the word before the caesura, with a word or group of syllables at the end of the line or another line

LYRIC the most common type of verse, composed to express the poet's personal emotions or sentiments; it may consist of solitary contemplation or be addressed to someone else

NARRATIVE a continuous account of an event or series of events

ODE a long lyric poem with an elevated style and formal stanzaic structure (rhymed or unrhymed), usually of a serious or meditative nature, treating progressively one dignified theme, often in the form of an address

PASTORAL a poem that idealizes the peaceful and simple lifestyle of people who live close to nature in the countryside

PINDARIC VERSE in Greek literature a poem designed for song, of various metres and of lofty style, patterned after the odes of the classical Greek poet, **Pindar**

SAPPHIC *a verse line consisting of five feet, of which the first, fourth, and fifth are trochees, the second is a spondee, and the third a dactyl*

'When the 'fierce 'north 'wind with his 'airy 'forces

Isaac Watts

NOTE: To find out more about trochees, spondee and dactyl see XV *VERSE FORM* p.160

SONNET *a 14 line lyric poem in which lines of iambic pentameter are linked by a formal rhyme scheme:*

The original **Petrarchan** or **Italian sonnet** comprises an octave (stanza of 8 lines) followed by a sestet (stanza of 6 lines) expressing successive phases of a single thought or sentiment (usually the octave establishes a problem or situation which is resolved in the sestet); the rhyme scheme for the octave is **abbaabba**, followed by two or three other rhymes in the sestet.

The **Shakespearean** or **English sonnet** comprises three quatrains (4-line groupings) and a final couplet (2 lines), rhyming **abab cdcd efef gg.** The thought structure of the English sonnet often follows the Petrarchan but sometimes variations on a theme are explored in the first three quatrains, followed by a concluding epigrammatic couplet.

Introductory stages

All that is required is that a candidate understands and empathizes with the material s/he has prepared. Encourage students to give very detailed consideration to the poetry and prose.

Candidates need to ask:

Q What would I have felt like if I had experienced this?

Q Is there anyone I know who has experienced this?

Q Have I ever felt this feeling?

Q Have I ever seen something like this?

NOTE: Improvisation is an invaluable means of developing a fuller understanding of material chosen. Trinity examiners often ask candidates to improvise within the discussion section of an examination.

Intermediate stages

Candidates will be required to have studied any theoretical topics listed in their particular examinations and relate their understanding to their presented work. For example, they should be able to identify deliberate pauses they used in their delivery, discuss why they used them, why they were needed and what would result if alternative approaches were taken. Where extracts have been chosen, candidates should be familiar with the complete work – particularly about what happens before and after the extract in question. Candidates must also think imaginatively about location and character relationships.

Advanced stages

Candidates should try to make some study of all the authors they have chosen – investigate some of what is known about them and look at their other works.

Candidates need to ask:

Q When was s/he writing?

Q Is this extract typical of his/her work?

Q Who else might have been writing at the same time?

Candidates need to understand the language and appreciate the style. Encourage them to think very carefully about how a knowledge and understanding of authors, history and theory can inform and enhance their performances.

After their examinations, students sometimes say things like, *"I didn't understand what the examiner wanted!"*

Do remember that examiners are not there to trick students. They want to provide students with opportunities to share their personal understanding of the prepared work together with other related knowledge and principles. If asked, examiners will readily rephrase a question or invitation.

Remember that an examiner is not only a specialist; s/he is a human being hoping to enjoy the work the student has prepared. Examiners want to be involved, inspired and entertained. Examiners work very hard and have to give 100% concentration and this can be quite tiring.

THINK ABOUT THIS: As one examiner said recently, *"When students are well prepared and full of vitality it is always a joy to meet them!"*

13   CONCLUSION

Always be very familiar with the syllabus and all its requirements.

Study the criteria because these will give some idea of what an examiner requires. Remember that these are guidelines and cannot cover all aspects.

Ensure that the candidate is well prepared and that s/he can present a confident performance.

Try to keep within the time limits because it is always upsetting for a student to be stopped part way through a performance – and if an examiner does NOT stop a candidate's over-running performance, s/he will be forced to shorten the discussion period automatically reducing the marks that can be earned in that section. Examiners are bound by time limits. Remember, if examinations over-run subsequent students and their teachers will normally complain because they will have to wait!

We very much hope that this book has given useful ideas for developing students' abilities. There are many other ways of stimulating students and encouraging them to gain a breadth of experience and knowledge. Experiment with new ideas and games – some will help, others will not.

Also, remember that students will learn far more if the teacher encourages and inspires them . . . . . so make sure that the lessons are fun!

Finally we list some useful books for further reading that will provide extra knowledge, ideas and stimulation.

FURTHER READING

Aaargh to Zizz 135 Drama Games
Talboys, Graeme K
Dramatic Lines Publishers
ISBN: 0953777057

Acting
Harrop, John
Taylor & Francis Books Ltd
ISBN: 0415059623

*Acting and Stage Movement: a Complete
Handbook for Amateurs and Professionals*
White, Marguerite and Battye, Edwin C
Meriwether Publishing Ltd
ISBN: 0916260305

*Acting Essentials: or Just Say Your Lines Like
You Mean Them and Don't Bump into the Scenery*
Golson, Alex
McGraw-Hill Education
ISBN: 0767422511

Acting Shakespeare
Barrie, Frank
Dramatic Lines Publishers
ISBN: 1904557104

Acting Skills
Morrison, Hugh
A & C Black Publishers Ltd
ISBN: 0713664231

Acting with Shakespeare: the Comedies
Suzman, Janet
Applause Theatre Book Publishers
ISBN: 1557832153

The Art of Acting: from Basic Exercises to Multidimensional Performances
Colyer, Carlton
Meriwether Publishing Ltd
ISBN: 0916260623

Body Voice Imagination
Zinder, David
Taylor & Francis Books Ltd
ISBN: 0878301518

Classical Acting
Morrison, Malcolm
A & C Black Publishers Ltd
ISBN: 0713640472

Clear Speech

Morrison, Malcolm

A & C Black Publishers Ltd

ISBN: 0713657936

Complete About Acting

Barkworth, Peter

Methuen Publishing Ltd

ISBN: 0413661105

The Complete Book of Speech Communication:
A Workbook of Ideas and Activities for Students
of Speech and Theatre

Marrs, Carol

Meriwether Publishing Ltd

ISBN: 0916260879

Does my Child Have a Speech Problem?

Martin, Katherine L

Chicago Review Press

ISBN: 1556523157

Effective Communication

Caputo, John; Palosaari, Jo and Pickering, Ken

Dramatic Lines Publishers

ISBN: 1904557139

English Phonetics and Phonology
Roach, Peter (University Of Reading)
Cambridge University Press
ISBN: 0521786134

Finding Your Voice
Houseman, Barbara
Nick Hern Books
ISBN: 1854596594

Freeing the Natural Voice
Linklater, Kristin
Quite Specific Media Group Ltd
ISBN: 0896760715

Gimson's Pronunciation of English
Cruttenden; Gimson
Arnold
ISBN: 0340806680

Guide to Practical Speech Training
Luck, Gordon
Vintage/Ebury (A Division of Random House Group)
ISBN: 0214200361

Ideal Voice and Speech Training
Parkin, Ken
Samuel French
ISBN: 0573090130

Impro
Johnstone, Keith
Methuen Publishing Ltd
ISBN: 041346430x

Improvisation for Theater
Spolin, Viola
Northwestern University Press
ISBN: 081014008X

An Introduction to the Art of Poetry
Fenton, James
Viking (Penguin Books)
ISBN: 0670911003

Mime
Hamblin, Kay
James Clarke & Co Ltd
ISBN: 071882461X

Mother Tongue
Bryson, Bill
Penguin Books Ltd
ISBN: 014014305x

Painless Speaking
Elizabeth, Mary
Barron's Educational Series
ISBN: 0764121472

The Physics of Speech
Fry, D B
Cambridge University Press
ISBN: 0521293790

Seeds of Speech
Aitchison, Jean (University of Oxford)
Cambridge University Press
ISBN: 0521785715

Speaking Rules!
Miyata, Cathy
Pembroke Publishing Ltd
ISBN: 155138132X

Speaking Shakespeare
Rodenburg, Patsy
Methuen Publishing Ltd
ISBN: 041376270X

Speaking Verse
Rodenburg, Patsy
Methuen Publishing Ltd
ISBN: 041370050X

Speech and Drama
Steiner, Rudolf
Anthroposophic Press
ISBN: 0854407103

Speech Chain
Denes, Peter B (Janus Systems Inc.) and Pinson, Elliot N
(At and T Bell Laboratories)
W H Freeman
ISBN: 0716723441

Speech for the Speaker
Miles-Brown, John
Peter Owen
ISBN: 0720607264

Speech for the Stage
Machlin, Evangeline
Routledge (Taylor & Francis Books Ltd)
ISBN: 0878300155

Speech Sounds
Ashby, Patricia
Taylor & Francis Books Ltd
ISBN: 0415085713

Stella Adler: the Art of Acting
Kissel, Howard
Applause Theatre Book Publishers
ISBN: 1557833737

Teaching Voice
Martin, Stephanie and Darnley, Lyn
Whurr Publishers Ltd
ISBN: 1897635192

Thinking About Plays
Pickering, Ken and Auckland-Lewis, Giles
Dramatic Lines Publishers
ISBN: 1904557147

Using Voice and Theatre in Therapy
Newham, Paul
Jessica Kingsley Publishers
ISBN: 1853025917

Voice and Speech in the Theatre
Turner, Clifford and Morrison, Malcolm
A & C Black Publishers Ltd
ISBN: 0713651938

Voice and the Actor
Berry, Cicely
Virgin Books
ISBN: 024552021x

Voice Book
Mccallion, Michael
Faber & Faber Ltd
ISBN: 0571195253

Your Voice and How to Use It
Berry, Cicely
Virgin Books
ISBN: 0863698263

All books may be ordered direct from:

DRAMATIC LINES   PO BOX 201   TWICKENHAM   TW2 5RQ   ENGLAND

freefone: 0800 5429570
t: 020 8296 9502
f: 020 8296 9503
e: mail@dramaticlinespublishers.co.uk
www.dramaticlines.co.uk

MONOLOGUES

| **THE SIEVE** | Heather Stephens |
| AND OTHER SCENES | ISBN 0 9522224 0 X |

The Sieve contains unusual short original monologues valid for junior acting examinations. The material in The Sieve has proved popular with winning entries worldwide in drama festival competitions. Although these monologues were originally written for the 8-14 year age range they have been used by adult actors for audition and performance pieces. Each monologue is seen through the eyes of a young person with varied subject matter including tough social issues such as fear, 'Television Spinechiller', senile dementia , 'Seen Through a Glass Darkly' and withdrawal from the world in 'The Sieve'. Other pieces include: 'A Game of Chicken', 'The Present', 'Balloon Race' and a widely used new adaptation of Hans Christian Andersen's 'The Little Match Girl' in monologue form.

| **CABBAGE** | Heather Stephens |
| AND OTHER SCENES | ISBN 0 9522224 5 0 |

Following the success of The Sieve, Heather Stephens has written an additional book of monologues with thought provoking and layered subject matter valid for junior acting examinations. The Cabbage monologues were originally written for the 8-14 year age range but have been used by adult actors for audition and performance pieces. The Aberfan slag-heap disaster issues are graphically confronted in 'Aberfan Prophecy' and 'The Surviving Twin' whilst humorous perceptions of life are observed by young people in 'The Tap Dancer' and 'Cabbage'. Other pieces include: 'The Dinner Party Guest', 'Nine Lives' and a new adaptation of Robert Browning's 'The Pied Piper' seen through the eyes of the crippled child.

ALONE IN MY ROOM
ORIGINAL MONOLOGUES

Ken Pickering
ISBN 0 9537770 0 6

This collection of short original monologues includes extracts from the author's longer works in addition to the classics. Provocative issues such as poverty and land abuse are explored in 'One Child at a Time', 'The Young Person Talks' and 'Turtle Island' with adaptations from 'Jane Eyre', Gulliver's Travels' and 'Oliver Twist' and well loved authors include Dostoyevsky. These monologues have a wide variety of applications including syllabus recommendation for various acting examinations. Each monologue has a brief background description and acting notes.

DUOLOGUES

PEARS

Heather Stephens
ISBN 0 9522224 6 9

These thought provoking and unusual short original duologues provide new material for speech and drama festival candidates in the 8-14 year age range. The scenes have also been widely used for junior acting examinations and in a variety of school situations and theatrical applications. Challenging topics in Pears include the emotive issues of child migration, 'Blondie', 'The Outback Institution' and bullying 'Bullies', other scenes examine friendship, 'The Best of Friends', 'The Row' and envy, 'Never the Bridesmaid'. New adaptations of part scenes from 'Peace' by Aristophanes and 'Oliver Twist' by Charles Dickens are also included.

TOGETHER NOW
ORIGINAL DUOLOGUES

Ken Pickering
ISBN 0 9537770 1 4

This collection of short duologues includes extracts from Ken Pickering's longer works together with new original pieces. The variety of experiences explored in the scenes can all be easily identified with, such as an awkward situation, 'You Tell Her', and the journey of self-knowledge in 'Gilgamesh', whilst 'Mobile phones', 'Sales' and 'Food' observe realistic situations in an interesting and perceptive way. Other duologues based on well-known stories include 'Snow White' and 'The Pilgrim's Progress'. Each piece has a brief background description and acting notes. The scenes have syllabus recommendation for a number of examination boards and wide variety of theatrical and school applications.

MONOLOGUES AND DUOLOGUES

SHAKESPEARE THE REWRITES

Claire Jones
ISBN 0 9522224 8 5

A collection of short monologues and duologues for female players. The scenes are from rewrites of Shakespeare plays from 1670 to the present day written by authors seeking to embellish original texts for performances, to add prequels or sequels or satisfy their own very personal ideas about production. This material is fresh and unusual and will provide exciting new audition and examination material. Comparisons with the original Shakespeare text are fascinating and this book will provide a useful contribution to Theatre Study work from GCSE to beyond 'A' level. Contributors include James Thurber (Macbeth) Arnold Wesker (Merchant of Venice) and Peter Ustinov (Romanoff and Juliet). The collection also includes a most unusual Japanese version of Hamlet.

RESOURCES

DRAMA LESSONS IN ACTION

Antoinette Line
ISBN 0 9522224 2 6

Resource material suitable for classroom and assembly use for teachers of junior and secondary age pupils. Lessons are taught through improvisation, these are not presented as 'model lessons' but provide ideas for adaptation and further development. Lessons include warm-up and speech exercises and many themes are developed through feelings such as timidity, resentfulness, sensitivity and suspicion. Material can be used by groups of varying sizes and pupils are asked to respond to texts from a diverse selection of well known authors including: Roald Dahl, Ogden Nash, John Betjeman, Ted Hughes, Michael Rosen, and Oscar Wilde.

AAARGH TO ZIZZ
135 DRAMA GAMES

Graeme Talboys
ISBN 0 9537770 5 7

This valuable resource material has been created by a drama teacher and used mostly in formal drama lessons but also in informal situations such as clubs and parties. The games are extremely flexible, from warm up to cool down, inspiration to conclusion and from deadly serious to purest fun and the wide variety ranges from laughing and rhythm activities to building a sentence and word association. Many games could be used as part of a PSHE programme together with activities connected with 'fair play'. The games are easily adapted and each has notes on setting up details of straightforward resources needed. All this material has been used with a wide range of young people in the 10 - 18 year age range.

DRAMA·DANCE·SINGING edited by John Nicholas
TEACHER RESOURCE BOOK ISBN 0 9537770 2 2

This collection of drama, dance and singing lesson activities has been drawn from a bank of ideas used by the Stagecoach Theatre Arts Schools teachers. Clearly presented lessons include speech and drama exercises, games and improvisations often developed as a response to emotions. Dance activities include warm-ups, basic dance positions, improvisations, versatile dance exercises and routines, while singing activities help to develop rhythm and notation as well as providing enjoyable games to develop the voice. Activities can be easily adapted for large or small group use and are suitable for 6 - 16 year olds in a fun yet challenging way.

MUSICAL PLAYS

THREE CHEERS FOR MRS BUTLER adapted by Vicky Ireland
ISBN 0 9537770 4 9

This versatile musical play about everyday school life is for anyone who has ever been to school. It features the poems and characters created by Allan Ahlberg with a foreword by Michael Rosen, songs by Colin Matthews and Steven Markwick and was first performed at the Polka Theatre for Children, London. The two acts of 40 minutes each can be performed by children, adults or a mixture of both and the play can be produced with a minimum cast of 7 or a large cast of any size, with or without music and songs, as well as having a wide variety of other musical and dramatic applications.

INTRODUCING OSCAR Veronica Bennetts
The Selfish Giant & The Happy Prince ISBN 0 9537770 3 0

Oscar Wilde's timeless stories for children have been chosen for adaptation because of the rich opportunities offered for imaginative exploration and the capacity to vividly illuminate many aspects of the human condition. The original dialogue, lyrics and music by Veronica Bennetts can be adapted and modified according to the needs of pupils, individual schools or drama groups. The Selfish Giant runs for 25 minutes and The Happy Prince for 1 hour 15 minutes. Both musical can be used for Trinity College, *London.* examinations and are ideal for end of term productions, for drama groups and primary and secondary schools.

A CD backing track for The Selfish Giant & The Happy Prince is available.

TEENAGE PLAYS

WHAT IS THE MATTER WITH MARY JANE?   Wendy Harmer
ISBN 0 9522224 4 2

This monodrama about a recovering anorexic and bulimic takes the audience into the painful reality of a young woman afflicted by eating disorders. The play is based on the personal experience of actress Sancia Robinson and has proved hugely popular in Australia. It is written with warmth and extraordinary honesty and the language, humour and style appeal to current youth culture. A study guide for teachers and students is included in this English edition ensuring that the material is ideal for use in the secondary school classroom and for PSHE studies, drama departments in schools and colleges in addition to amateur and professional performance.

X-STACY
Margery Forde
ISBN 0 9522224 9 3

Margery Forde's powerful play centres on the rave culture and illicit teenage drug use and asks tough questions about family, friends and mutual responsibilities. The play has proved hugely successful in Australia and this English edition is published with extensive teachers' notes by Helen Radian, Lecturer of Drama at Queensland University of Technology, to enrich its value for the secondary school classroom, PSHE studies, English and drama departments.

ASSEMBLIES

ASSEMBLIES! ASSEMBLIES! ASSEMBLIES!   Kryssy Hurley
ISBN 0 9537770 6 5

These teacher-led assemblies require minimum preparation and have been written by a practising teacher to involve small or large groups. Each assembly lasts 15-20 minutes and is suitable for Key Stages 2 and 3. There are 12 for each term and these explore many PSHE and Citizenship issues including bullying, racism, friendship, co-operation, feeling positive, making responsible choices and decisions, school rules and laws outside school. All have the following sections: *Resource and Organisation, What To Do, Reflection Time and Additional Resources and Activities.* The assemblies are both enjoyable and informative for pupils participating and audiences alike.

SUGAR ON SUNDAYS
AND OTHER PLAYS

Andrew Gordon
ISBN 0 9522224 3 4

A collection of six one act plays bringing history alive through drama. History is viewed through the eyes of ordinary people and each play is packed with details about everyday life, important events and developments of the period. The plays can be used as classroom drama, for school performances and group acting examinations and also as shared texts for the literacy hour. The plays are suitable for children from Key Stage 2 upwards and are 40-50 minutes in length and explore Ancient Egypt, Ancient Greece, Anglo-Saxon and Viking Times, Victorian Britain and the Second World War. A glossary of key words helps to develop children's historical understanding of National Curriculum History Topics and the plays provide opportunities for children to enjoy role-play and performance.

DRAMATIC LINES HANDBOOKS in association with

Trinity, The International Examinations Board

SPEECH AND DRAMA

ISBN 1 904557 15 5

Ann Jones and Robert Cheeseman

▯

THINKING ABOUT PLAYS

ISBN 1 904557 14 7

Ken Pickering and Giles Auckland-Lewis

▯

EFFECTIVE COMMUNICATION

ISBN 1 904557 13 9

John Caputo, Jo Palosaari and Ken Pickering

▯

ACTING SHAKESPEARE FOR AUDITIONS AND EXAMINATIONS

ISBN 1 904557 10 4

Frank Barrie

▯

PREPARING FOR YOUR DIPLOMA IN DRAMA AND SPEECH

ISBN 1 904557 11 2

Kirsty N Findlay and Ken Pickering

▯

MUSICAL THEATRE

ISBN 1 904557 12 0

Gerry Tebbutt